MATTHEW 1–2/ LUKE 1–2

Joy to the World

A Guided Discovery for Groups and Individuals

Louise Perrotta

LOYOLAPRESS.

CHICAGO

LOYOLAPRESS.

3441 N. ASHLAND AVENUE
CHICAGO, ILLINOIS 60657
(800) 621-1008
WWW.LOYOLABOOKS.ORG

Nihil Obstat	*Imprimatur*
Reverend John G. Lodge, S.S.L., S.T.D.	Most Reverend Edwin M. Conway, D.D.
Censor Deputatus	Vicar General
September 9, 2003	Archdiocese of Chicago
	September 10, 2003

The *Nihil Obstat* and *Imprimatur* are official declarations that a book is free of doctrinal and moral error. No implication is contained therein that those who have granted the *Nihil Obstat* and *Imprimatur* agree with the content, opinions, or statements expressed. Nor do they assume any legal responsibility associated with publication.

The Scripture quotations contained herein are from the New Revised Standard Version Bible: Catholic Edition, copyright © 1993 and 1989 by the Division of Christian Education of the National Council of the Churches of Christ in the U.S.A. Used by permission. All rights reserved. Subheadings in Scripture quotations have been added by Louise Perrotta.

The Greek text of the excerpts from the two sermons of St. John Chrysostom (p. 23) can be found in J.-P. Migne, ed., *Patrologiae Graeca (*Paris, 1982). The English translation here is from Francis L. Filas, S.J., *Joseph: The Man Closest to Jesus* (Boston: St. Paul Editions, 1962).

For information on the "Book of Life" (p. 33), write to The Church of the Holy Innocents, 128 West 37th St., New York, New York 10018; call (212) 279-5861, extension 24; or visit www.innocents.com. Project Rachel can be contacted at the National Office of Post-Abortion Reconciliation and Healing (NOPARH), P.O. Box 070477, Milwaukee, Wisconsin 53207-0477; 1-800-5WE-CARE; www.marquette.edu/rachels.

Alfred Delp's meditation (p. 43) is from *The Prison Meditations of Father Alfred Delp* (New York: Herder and Herder, 1963).

Bertha Spafford Vester's reminiscences (p. 63) are taken from her book *Our Jerusalem: An American Family in the Holy City, 1881–1949* (Jerusalem: The American Colony/Ariel Publishing House, 1988). To obtain information about the Spafford Children's Center, write to 4550 132nd Ave., N.E., Bellevue, Washington 98005; call (425) 885-4926; or visit www.spafford-kids.org.

The excerpt from Charles de Foucauld (p. 73) is from Jean-François Six, ed., J. Holland Smith, trans., *The Spiritual Autobiography of Charles de Foucauld* (Ijamsville, Md.: The Word Among Us Press, 2003). For information about various groups within the spiritual family of Charles de Foucauld, visit www.jesuscaritas.info.

The excerpt from Dorothy Day (p. 74) is from "Room for Christ," *Catholic Worker*, December 1945, 2. It is reprinted from the Dorothy Day Library on the Web at www.catholicworker.org/dorothyday.

The excerpt from Edith Stein (p. 75) is from Hilda C. Graef, ed., *Writings of Edith Stein* (Westminster, Md.: Newman Press, 1956).

Interior design by Kay Hartmann/Communique Design
Illustration by Charise Mericle Harper

ISBN 0-8294-1541-6

Printed in the United States of America
04 05 06 07 08 09 10 11 Bang 10 9 8 7 6 5 4 3 2 1

Contents

How to Use This Guide

You might compare the Bible to a national park. The park is so large that you could spend months, even years, getting to know it. But a brief visit, if carefully planned, can be enjoyable and worthwhile. In a few hours you can drive through the park and pull over at a handful of sites. At each stop you can get out of the car, take a short trail through the woods, listen to the wind blowing through the trees, get a feel for the place.

In this booklet we'll drive through a small portion of the Bible—the stories revolving around Jesus' birth and early years—reading six excerpts from the Gospel according to Matthew and the Gospel according to Luke. At those points we'll proceed on foot, taking a leisurely walk through the selected passages. After each discussion we'll get back in the car and take the highway to the next stop.

This guide provides everything you need to explore the readings from Matthew's and Luke's Gospels in six discussions— or to do a six-part exploration on your own. The introduction on page 6 will prepare you to get the most out of your reading. The weekly sections provide explanations that highlight what the Gospels mean for us today. Equally important, each section supplies questions that will launch you into fruitful discussion, helping you to both investigate the Gospels for yourself and learn from one another. If you're using the booklet by yourself, the questions will spur your personal reflection.

Each discussion is meant to be a *guided discovery*.

Guided. None of us is equipped to read the Bible without help. We read the Bible *for* ourselves but not *by* ourselves. Scripture was written to be understood and applied in the community of faith. So each week "A Guide to the Reading," drawing on the work of both modern biblical scholars and Christian writers of the past, supplies background and explanations. The guide will help you grasp the message of the Gospel readings. Think of it as a friendly park ranger who points out noteworthy details and explains what you're looking at so you can appreciate things for yourself.

Discovery. The purpose is for *you* to interact with Matthew's and Luke's Gospels. "Questions for Careful Reading" is a tool to help you dig into the text and examine it carefully. "Questions for Application" will help you consider what these words mean for your life here and now. Each week concludes with an "Approach to Prayer" section that helps you respond to God's word. Supplementary "Living Tradition" and "Saints in the Making" sections offer the thoughts and experiences of Christians past and present. By showing what the Gospel accounts of Jesus' birth and early years have meant to others, these sections will help you consider what they mean for you.

How long are the discussion sessions? We've assumed you will have about an hour and a half when you get together. If you have less time, you'll find that most of the elements can be shortened somewhat.

Is homework necessary? You will get the most out of your discussions if you read the weekly material and prepare answers to the questions in advance of each meeting. If participants are not able to prepare, have someone read the "Guide to the Reading" sections aloud to the group at the points where they appear.

What about leadership? If you happen to have a world-class biblical scholar in your group, by all means ask him or her to lead the discussions. In the absence of any professional Scripture scholars, or even accomplished amateur biblical scholars, you can still have a first-class Bible discussion. Choose two or three people to take turns as facilitators, and have everyone read "Suggestions for Bible Discussion Groups" (page 76) before beginning.

Does everyone need a guide? a Bible? Everyone in the group will need his or her own copy of this booklet. It contains the text of the portions of the Gospels that are discussed, so a Bible is not absolutely necessary—but each participant will find it useful to have one. You should have at least one Bible on hand for your discussions. (See page 80 for recommendations.)

How do we get started? Before you begin, take a look at the suggestions for Bible discussion groups (page 76) or individuals (page 79).

Finding Mercy at the Manger

My husband returns from walking the dog and reports that the trumpeter swan living at the nearby pond is trying to drown a gosling from the family of Canada geese also living there. It's absurd to feel disappointed, but I do. The swan is so majestically beautiful and its raucous call so amusing—was I perhaps expecting behavior to match? Something nobler than "nature, red in tooth and claw"?

I go online to scan the headlines. Less absurdly, I'm dismayed at the quantity of red splashed about there, not all of it deriving from "nature." An earthquake that leaves sixteen hundred people dead and seven thousand injured. A fatal eighty-five-car pile-up on a fogbound freeway. The latest sensationalized murder. A tragic shelling error that kills eleven members of an Iraqi family. I go away haunted by its elderly patriarch's lament that "our home is an empty place. We who are left are like wild animals—all we can do is cry, and cry out."

Against the dark background of suffering, sin, and struggle that make up so much of life, it can sometimes feel as if the whole world is a sad and empty place resounding with desperate cries. The first two chapters of Matthew's and Luke's Gospels proclaim otherwise. They headline "Good News of Great Joy for All People!" (Luke 2:10). They say it's not a dirge we should be singing, but a carol: "Joy to the world! The Lord has come!"

Especially during Advent, and whenever we recite the Creed at Mass, we are reminded that this Lord, Jesus, "will come again in glory to judge the living and the dead." At the end of time, he will establish a kingdom of perfect peace and justice that will have no end. On that day, "the wolf shall live with the lamb" (Isaiah 11:6)—and the swan, no doubt, will coexist peacefully with the goose. All wrongs will be set right. Every tear will be wiped away. Death will be no more. This glorious Second Coming will be the perfect finish to the story of the humble first coming recounted in the infancy narratives (as Matthew 1–2 and Luke 1–2 are often called): "Joy to the world! The Lord *will* come!"

Many of us find it relatively easy to sing a jubilant "Joy to the World" on Christmas Day, as we celebrate Jesus' lowly first coming. Once the festivities cease, however, it is not always so easy to live in the joyful reality that "the Lord *has* come." Yet here is an event with year-round, day-in-day-out implications for us. How fully have we understood this mystery of God becoming human, of the Incarnation? And what does it mean to celebrate the coming of the Lord into our still struggling world?

Each evangelist unfolds this mystery of Jesus' coming in his own particular way. All four offer a perspective on what Jesus did and said during his public ministry and, especially, on his suffering and death. These core events formed the substance of the earliest Christian preaching (see Peter's sermon in Acts 10:36–41, for example, and Paul's in 1 Corinthians 15:3–5). But it is only Matthew and Luke who fill out the picture of Jesus' earthly life with some snapshots from his early years. Taking up just four of the eighty-nine chapters that constitute the four Gospels, these birth and infancy scenes (plus one view of Jesus at age twelve) have had an impact and influence all out of proportion to their length. Certainly, today's non-Christian knows more about Christmas than about Easter.

At least part of the story's great appeal is that it presents the whole gospel message in a concentrated form that stirs the heart. Kneeling at the manger, we come face-to-face with God's answer to pain and injustice. The answer is a child—a human being at the most dependent, vulnerable stage of life. That this child is also the "Son of God" (Luke 1:35) is a reality so awesome that we can only marvel at the mystery. Here is divine mercy taken flesh, the evidence that God hears our cries and sees our suffering. Here is the proof of his great love for "those who sit in darkness and in the shadow of death" (Luke 1:79). God could have saved us from a distance, I suppose. Instead, he came in person in Jesus—"'Emmanuel,' which means, 'God is with us'" (Matthew 1:23). Through the Holy Spirit, by whom Jesus was conceived (Matthew 1:20; Luke 1:35), he remains with us still.

You'll notice that there is nothing overly sweet or senti-mental in the way Luke and Matthew present the events surround-ing Jesus' birth and early years. The Incarnation came at a high price, and their telling reveals it. There is the fact that the King of kings enters into the world as one of the lowly, into a family without power or wealth. Matthew says they are political refugees and that Jesus' adoptive father is a carpenter (2:13–15; 13:55). Luke stresses the poverty of Jesus' birth and of his ceremonial presentation in the temple, where the family offers what their budget can afford: not a sheep but two birds (2:7, 24; Leviticus 12:8). Certain episodes in particular reveal that the crib stands in the shadow of the cross. In Matthew, this is especially evident in the enmity of Herod, the local ruler of the time, and his massacre of the boys of Bethlehem. In Luke, Simeon's prophetic words to Mary sound a somber note, which reechoes in the later episode of the finding of Jesus.

By evoking such themes, Matthew and Luke point us ahead to the events of Jesus' adult life and prepare us to enter into the drama of his death and resurrection. At the same time, they invite us to cast a backward glance over the road already traveled—that is, the history of God's dealings with his chosen people.

Through direct quotes and subtle allusions, the two evangelists connect Jesus with Israel's past and reveal him to be the fulfillment of all its hopes. They recall its great figures: Abraham and David in particular, but also Moses, the patriarch Joseph, the prophet Samuel, and others. They recap pivotal moments in Israel's history: God's covenant with Abraham to make him a great nation and a blessing to all peoples; the exodus from Egypt and deliverance from the slavery of Pharaoh (to whom King Herod bears some resemblance); God's promise to give one of David's heirs an everlasting kingdom; and Israel's captivity and exile in foreign lands, when the voices of prophets like Isaiah held out hope of future restoration.

The Guides to the Readings will point out some of these Old Testament echoes. If you have the time, you'll benefit from examining some of the footnotes and cross-references in a good study Bible. (Mary's and Zechariah's prayers of praise are especially rich: Luke 1:46–55, 68–79; or for a full immersion into Israel's history, try the genealogy that opens Matthew's Gospel: 1:1–17.) The greater your awareness of these elements, the more you will appreciate Luke's and Matthew's artistry, to say nothing of their example of pondering Scripture. The message they most want to convey, however, is that in Jesus, God has delivered on his every promise and that this is great good news for *all* the world's peoples (Luke 2:29–32).

Like all good writers, the two evangelists tailored their message to fit their first readers—Jewish Christians, in Matthew's case, and gentile Christians, in Luke's. Writing some decades after Jesus' death, neither author witnessed the events he reported, though Luke mentions eyewitnesses as the source of his information (1:2). For the narratives about Jesus' birth that we will be reading, Matthew and Luke seem to have drawn on separate traditions and did not depend on each other as they wrote. Given the unrelatedness of their sources, the remarkable agreement of these two independently constructed narratives is an important indicator of their reliability. In both Gospels:

◆ Jesus is conceived by Mary, a virgin, by the power of the Holy Spirit. She is engaged to Joseph, but they are not living together.

◆ Jesus' birth is announced by an angel (to Joseph in Matthew's account, to Mary in Luke's), who identifies the child to be born as Savior and specifies the name he is to be given.

◆ Joseph and Mary are living together by the time Jesus is born in Bethlehem, during the reign of Herod the Great.

◆ Joseph is of the lineage of David; through him, Jesus is recognized as a son of David.

◆ Jesus grows up in Galilee.

Luke and Matthew agree so completely on these basics that either we hardly notice the differences in their stories or we unconsciously form composite pictures that smooth them over. The Christmas crèche is a good example. Ever since 1223, when St. Francis of Assisi had this happy inspiration, we have been combining, without a second thought, Matthew's star and Magi with Luke's manger, angels, and shepherds. (The ox and donkey may be from Isaiah 1:3.)

There are other differences as well. Only Matthew tells us about Joseph's dreams, Herod's ordering of the massacre of the babies in Bethlehem, and the holy family's flight to Egypt. Only Luke reports the annunciations to Zechariah and to Mary, her visit to Elizabeth, the census, the presentation of Jesus, and the Passover visit to Jerusalem when Jesus is found in the temple. Simeon and Anna, as well as three beautiful "canticles," or spoken prayers of praise, also come to us by way of Luke (1:46–55, 68–79; 2:29–32).

As exemplified by the Christmas crib, some of the unique features of Matthew's and Luke's accounts fit together quite nicely. Others can be harmonized only by devising ingenious solutions that often strain credulity. Sometimes, the two accounts do seem to stand in tension, as in the Evangelists' presentation of Jesus' family tree (we will look at Matthew's only; Luke's, which is different, appears in 3:23–38).

There are questions, too, about the degree to which Luke and Matthew allowed themselves some poetic license in telling their stories. Like other authors of ancient times, they were less preoccupied than we are with exact facts, figures, and dates. Exploring such historical issues, which are not central to the infancy narratives' basic message, would take us beyond the scope of a short, introductory book such as this. If you are interested in pursuing them, however, you'll find ample reading in the resource materials listed on page 80.

When it comes to noncritical discrepancies like these, I like the "live and let live" approach that the Church Father Origen proposed in the third century. Speaking about all the Gospel writers, he advised: "But let these four agree with one another concerning certain basic things revealed to them by the Spirit and let them disagree a little concerning other things."

If we can put up with a little disagreement of this type, we will find that our vision of Jesus' early years is richer for being "binocular." Using their particular Holy Spirit–inspired perceptions and skills, Matthew and Luke have each come up with a uniquely beautiful approach to their subject.

Matthew opens with a genealogy (1:1–17). This probably would not have been our opening of choice, but in his hands, it becomes a fascinating living extension ladder leading up to Jesus. The names are arranged in three sections, each one covering a period of Israel's history. Level one begins with Abraham and continues through the patriarchs (Abraham's immediate descendants) up to the kings of Israel. Level two starts with

King David and ends with the last of the kings of Israel, Jechoniah. Level three lists mostly people who are mentioned nowhere else in Scripture before finally moving up to Joseph, Mary, and Jesus.

His ladder complete, Matthew presents the rest of the story of Jesus' origins in five scenes that reveal him to be the fulfillment of the ancient prophecies about the Messiah—the Christ, or "Anointed One," commissioned to spearhead God's kingdom on earth. As in a slide show, one picture follows another: the annunciation to Joseph and birth of Jesus, the visit of the Magi, the flight into Egypt, the massacre of the innocents, the return from Egypt. And just so we don't miss the point, each episode either ends or climaxes with an Old Testament quotation that stands out like a photo caption and is announced by a phrase like "all this took place to fulfill what had been spoken by the Lord through the prophet" or "so it has been written by the prophet."

While Jesus is the focus of Matthew's narrative, it is Joseph who stands out as the hero. Consistently and faithfully obedient to God, he is the type of *doer* whom Jesus will commend: hearing God's word, he acts on it (Matthew 1:24; 2:14–15, 21–23; 7:21; 21:28–32). Joseph is also the "righteous" man who respects and loves the Jewish law and interprets it with mercy (Matthew 1:19).

To understand the decision Joseph is struggling with as Matthew's story opens (in 1:18–24—we'll look at this passage in Week 1), it helps to know something about wedding customs in first-century Palestine. Basically, marriages took place in two stages. The first was an engagement ratified by witnesses at the bride's house. This was a formal declaration of intent to marry; afterward, the man and woman were legally considered husband and wife and were bound to matrimonial fidelity, though they did not yet live together. Mary's pregnancy comes to light during this time (Matthew 1:18; Luke 1:27). The second stage, which took place about a year later, was the wedding ceremony, in which the bride was escorted from her family's home to the groom's. Most marriages were arranged by families, and the usual age for betrothal was probably twelve or thirteen for women and a few years older for men.

What a different presentation we find when we turn to Luke! Instead of projecting a slide-show sequence of scenes, Luke uses a split-screen effect to depict parallel episodes from the lives of John the Baptist and Jesus. Similar events appear side by side: on both screens, an angel announces an extraordinary conception and a son is born, named, circumcised, and revealed as a divinely sent agent of salvation. But the scenes are hardly a matching set, for each pair clearly presents the superiority of the Savior over his herald.

Luke says that John will be "great in the sight of the Lord." Jesus will be "great" because he is "the Son of the Most High" (Luke 1:15, 32). John will be filled with the Spirit "even before his birth," from the time he is in his mother's womb, but Jesus will be so from conception (Luke 1:15, 35). "Many" will rejoice at John's birth, but Jesus' coming will be "good news of great joy for all the people" (Luke 1:14; 2:10). John will "make ready a people prepared for the Lord"; Jesus will rule them as the Son of David whose kingdom will have no end (Luke 1:17, 33).

In Luke's Gospel, it is Mary who stands out. She, not Joseph, is the one who receives the announcement of Jesus' birth. She is praised by Gabriel and by Elizabeth and receives a prophetic word from Simeon. She declares God's faithfulness in a joyful, powerful canticle. In a more subdued moment twelve years later, it is she who speaks up to question her Son (Luke 2:48). Luke presents Mary as the one who retains and reflects on the amazing events surrounding her Son's coming and who finally understands what they signify. (In the Acts of the Apostles, the sequel to Luke's Gospel, Mary is present among the believers at Pentecost: 1:14.)

This brings us back to our original question: how fully have we grasped the implications of the Incarnation? Speaking for myself, I have to admit that when I come to the manger with some disturbing news article in hand or with my personal problems prominently in mind, I often feel a sense of kinship with Jesus' slow-to-understand disciples. Just before his ascension into heaven, they were still asking, "Lord, is this the time when you will restore the kingdom to Israel?" (Acts 1:6). Despite everything they had seen and heard—and right up until the day of Pentecost—they still expected and wanted him to ascend an earthly throne.

In a way, that's what I want too. "Reveal your justice, Lord!" (But be extremely merciful to me.) "Overthrow the proud and the rich!" (Surely I'm not one of those.) "Establish your kingdom fully in our world!" (About time us Christians got some respect around here.)

The poverty of the manger exposes such self-centeredness. Like the cross, it acts as a powerful light by which "the inner thoughts of many will be revealed" (Luke 2:35). The Child lying in that humble bed is indeed the King who will return in glory to execute justice, raise up the lowly, and establish an everlasting reign. Right now, though, his kingdom is still operating in the hidden, humble, personally costly mode of mercy.

Will I align myself with this kingdom? Will I open myself to the Holy Spirit, who transforms and empowers people to live the kingdom life and express it to one another? Will I allow him to purify my desires so that I can long and work for justice in an unselfish way and be a messenger of God's mercy in my world?

As we wrestle with these questions, it makes sense to turn to Mary. She is the one who understood and proclaimed that mercy is God's basic operating principle: "His mercy is . . . from generation to generation" (Luke 1:50). At both the manger and the cross, when God's mercy was manifested in a special way, Mary was right there, aligning herself with it. She is the mother of mercy, interceding for us so that we also might pray for mercy and "do mercy."

Pope John Paul II has pointed out that in every time and historical period—but "especially at a moment as critical as our own"—we have "the right and the duty to appeal to the God of mercy 'with loud cries' (Hebrews 5:7)." In fact, he said, "these 'loud cries' should be the mark of the Church of our times, cries uttered to God to implore his mercy" (*Rich in Mercy,* section 15, paragraph 1).

If we kneel at the manger uttering these cries in alternation with stanzas of "Joy to the World," we won't be off the mark.

SURPRISES AND EXPECTATIONS

Questions to Begin

15 minutes
Use a question or two to get warmed up for the reading.

---

1   Has anyone ever done research on your family tree? Were there any surprises?

---

2   Describe how you felt the last time you were touched by an angel.

---

3   When you decide to sleep on a problem instead of making a decision right away, what generally happens?
❑ I wake up knowing exactly what should be done.
❑ I toss and turn and don't sleep a wink.
❑ I think of factors I had overlooked.
❑ I feel guilty about procrastinating.
❑ I feel even more uncertain about what to do.
❑ I can't even remember the problem when morning comes.

5 minutes
Read the passage aloud. Let individuals take turns reading
paragraphs. (Don't worry about stumbling over some of the
names in the genealogy. Just do the best you can.)

The Reading: Matthew 1:1–25

A Family Tree with Surprises

[1] An account of the genealogy of Jesus the Messiah, the son of David, the son of Abraham.

[2] Abraham was the father of Isaac, and Isaac the father of Jacob, and Jacob the father of Judah and his brothers, [3] and Judah the father of Perez and Zerah by Tamar, and Perez the father of Hezron, and Hezron the father of Aram, [4] and Aram the father of Aminadab, and Aminadab the father of Nahshon, and Nahshon the father of Salmon, [5] and Salmon the father of Boaz by Rahab, and Boaz the father of Obed by Ruth, and Obed the father of Jesse, [6] and Jesse the father of King David.

And David was the father of Solomon by the wife of Uriah, [7] and Solomon the father of Rehoboam, and Rehoboam the father of Abijah, and Abijah the father of Asaph, [8] and Asaph the father of Jehoshaphat, and Jehoshaphat the father of Joram, and Joram the father of Uzziah, [9] and Uzziah the father of Jotham, and Jotham the father of Ahaz, and Ahaz the father of Hezekiah, [10] and Hezekiah the father of Manasseh, and Manasseh the father of Amos, and Amos the father of Josiah, [11] and Josiah the father of Jechoniah and his brothers, at the time of the deportation to Babylon.

[12] And after the deportation to Babylon: Jechoniah was the father of Salathiel, and Salathiel the father of Zerubbabel, [13] and Zerubbabel the father of Abiud, and Abiud the father of Eliakim, and Eliakim the father of Azor, [14] and Azor the father of Zadok, and Zadok the father of Achim, and Achim the father of Eliud, [15] and Eliud the father of Eleazar, and Eleazar the father of Matthan, and Matthan the father of Jacob, [16] and Jacob the father of Joseph the husband of Mary, of whom Jesus was born, who is called the Messiah.

[17] So all the generations from Abraham to David are fourteen generations; and from David to the deportation to Babylon, fourteen generations; and from the deportation to Babylon to the Messiah, fourteen generations.

The Annunciation to Joseph

¹⁸ Now the birth of Jesus the Messiah took place in this way. When his mother Mary had been engaged to Joseph, but before they lived together, she was found to be with child from the Holy Spirit. ¹⁹ Her husband Joseph, being a righteous man and unwilling to expose her to public disgrace, planned to dismiss her quietly. ²⁰ But just when he had resolved to do this, an angel of the Lord appeared to him in a dream and said, "Joseph, son of David, do not be afraid to take Mary as your wife, for the child conceived in her is from the Holy Spirit. ²¹ She will bear a son, and you are to name him Jesus, for he will save his people from their sins." ²² All this took place to fulfill what had been spoken by the Lord through the prophet:

> ²³ "Look, the virgin shall conceive and bear a son,
>   and they shall name him Emmanuel,"

which means, "God is with us." ²⁴ When Joseph awoke from sleep, he did as the angel of the Lord commanded him; he took her as his wife, ²⁵ but had no marital relations with her until she had borne a son; and he named him Jesus.

Questions for Careful Reading

10 minutes
Choose questions according to your interest and time.

1 Can you think of reasons why Matthew might have chosen to begin his Gospel with a list of names? Identify the names you are familiar with. What do you know about these people?

2 The genealogy rolls on with a certain rhythm—until Matthew 1:16. What changes? Why is the change significant?

3 Matthew does not spell out Joseph's emotional reaction to the dilemma he faces. How would you fill in the blanks?

4 How does Matthew bring out the fact that Jesus is the Son of God? Is Joseph a father in any meaningful sense?

5 What do Joseph's actions reveal about his character? What overall picture of Joseph emerges from this reading? Back up your statements with specific references.

A Guide to the Reading

If participants have not read this section already, read it aloud. Otherwise go on to "Questions for Application."

You can almost hear the groans resounding throughout the church when the Gospel reading at Mass turns out to be "the genealogy of Jesus the Messiah" (Matthew 1:1). And yet this list of names contains fascinating clues about the identity of Jesus. Its very presence makes a statement: Jesus didn't just suddenly show up like some superhero from outer space. He is truly one of us, a real person with a family tree—and even some skeletons in the closet (Manasseh, to name only one: Matthew 1:10; see 2 Kings 21:1–16).

Two titles situate Jesus within the story of Israel. "Son of David" signals that he is the Messiah foretold by Israel's prophets, the fulfillment of God's promise to establish a descendant of King David as ruler of an everlasting kingdom (2 Samuel 7:12–13). "Son of Abraham" recalls God's promise to bless all nations through Abraham's posterity (Genesis 22:18).

In three sections of fourteen names apiece (Matthew 1:17), the genealogy recalls key moments in Israel's history. Its neat symmetry suggests that God has been at work behind the scenes, orchestrating events for the Savior's appearance.

The genealogy also reveals a God of surprises. Rather unusually, foremothers appear (Matthew 1:3, 5–6)—not Israel's great matriarchs but four women who were seen as foreigners. Their presence announces that non-Jews, too, have reason to hail the Messiah. But the women also add a jarring note, given the circumstances of their motherhood: Tamar posed as a prostitute; Rahab was one; Ruth got herself a husband in an unconventional way; Bathsheba was drawn into an adulterous relationship with David (Genesis 38; Joshua 2; Ruth 3–4; 2 Samuel 11). "These mothers foreshadow the irregular birth of Jesus," says New Testament scholar Daniel Harrington, S.J. They "set up the reader to expect the unexpected."

Even so, the careful reader is startled by the abrupt disappearance of the refrain "was the father of" as the family history reaches Joseph. As it turns out, he is "the husband of Mary, of whom Jesus was born" (Matthew 1:16)—not somebody's father but somebody's spouse.

Is this genealogical chain missing its last critical link, then? No—the story of Jesus' birth reveals that he is of David's lineage, though in an unusual way. On the one hand, Jesus has no human father; he is conceived "from the Holy Spirit" (Matthew 1:18). On the other hand, Joseph's fatherhood is real and determinative: Israelite families were based on legal, not biological, paternity. By obeying the angel's command to name Mary's child, Joseph formally acknowledges Jesus as his son and gives him his own "son of David" status (Matthew 1:1, 20).

This naming of Jesus is the climax of a drama starring Joseph. Introduced as a "righteous" follower of the Mosaic law (Matthew 1:19), he must deal with the fact that the woman he loves is pregnant, but not by him. A rigid legalist would have implemented the law by charging Mary with unchastity in a public trial (Deuteronomy 22:13–24; Numbers 5:11–31). By doing this, Joseph could have cleared himself of responsibility for the untimely pregnancy without having to return the dowry. But this just man finds a more compassionate way to fulfill the law—by dismissing Mary "quietly" (Matthew 1:19), perhaps with a simple certificate of divorce that does not need to be witnessed and does not mention adultery.

The angel's nighttime annunciation causes Joseph to reverse direction. It is like a spotlight illuminating Jesus' identity—and also the fatherly role that Joseph is to play.

Is Joseph relieved at learning that Mary's child is "from the Holy Spirit" (Matthew 1:20) and that he can resume plans to share his life with his beloved? Is he startled that the angel interprets the name "Jesus"—"the Lord saves" was its popular meaning—in terms of salvation from sin (Matthew 1:21), not in terms of the military victories expected of the Messiah? What does Joseph make of the reference to Emmanuel, which evokes a prophecy he would have known (Matthew 1:23; Isaiah 7:14)? Does he realize that his marriage will be intimate but without its normal physical expression? (In the Greek text of Matthew's Gospel, the "until" in 1:25 does not imply that the couple had marital relations after Jesus' birth.)

The drama ends with Joseph doing exactly as commanded. Whatever questions he may have, he accepts Mary "in all the mystery of her motherhood," as Pope John Paul II has said.

Questions for Application

40 minutes
Choose questions according to your interest and time.

1 Jesus' family tree includes well-known figures and people not mentioned anywhere else in Scripture. What might this suggest about your own family history? about your place in God's plan of salvation?

2 George Montague suggests that Matthew's genealogy challenges our notions of achievement and self-worth. "Do we get our identity from what we do—or from our relationships? Is my importance something I have to prove or merit—or something I begin with because of the galaxy of relationships into which I am born?" What do you think?

3 Joseph was concerned about both obeying God's law and showing mercy. What can you learn from his example about how to approach some of your relationships with other people?

4 Jesus is Emmanuel, "God is with us"—not a figure from the past but someone who accompanies us today. Is this promise a reality for you? Where in your life do you meet Jesus? How could you grow in awareness that he is with you?

5 Do you generally have the expectation that God stands ready to guide you through your dilemmas? Are you deliberating over any particular problem right now? What could help you receive God's direction?

6 People who didn't know about Joseph's dream were perhaps scandalized that he went through with the wedding. Have you ever taken flak from people for doing something you knew was right? (When have you hastily criticized someone else's behavior?)

7 For personal reflection: Right from the beginning, Jesus loved us so much that he didn't hesitate to identify with the less-than-perfect human beings in his own extended family. Is your own love as humble and generous? Do you put conditions on your love or withhold approval depending on people's actions?

Love the Bible and wisdom will love you; love it and it will preserve you; honor it and it will embrace you; these are the jewels which you should wear on your breast and in your ears.

St. Jerome, *Letter to Demetrias*

Approach to Prayer

15 minutes
Use this approach—or create your own!

◆ Let each person silently consider the needs of their family members. Allow an opportunity for participants to offer aloud any requests they wish to mention. After each petition, pray together:

Jesus, Emmanuel, come into our families, bringing your forgiveness and help.

End with an Our Father or with this prayer to the patron saint of families, adapted from a prayer by Pope Leo XIII:

We come to you, St. Joseph, remembering your tender love for Mary, the Virgin Mother of God, and for the child Jesus. We entrust ourselves and each member of our families to your love as well. Pray for us, watchful guardian of the holy family. Keep us under your protection so that, guided by your example and supported by your help, we may each be enabled to lead a holy life, die a happy death, and enter into the joy of heaven.

A Living Tradition

Joseph the Just

This section is a supplement for individual reading.

Why did Joseph decide he should divorce Mary (Matthew 1:19)? Did he think she had conceived through adultery or rape—and that he was therefore bound to "purge the evil," as the Mosaic law directed (Deuteronomy 22:21)? Or did he know, even before his dream, that Mary's pregnancy was miraculous—and draw back out of reverent awe? The first reason seems more likely (why would the angel tell Joseph something he already knew?) and was the view of most Church Fathers, including Justin and Augustine. But some, like Basil and Jerome, opted for the second. Whatever their interpretation of Joseph's motives, however, these early writers had high praise for this "just man" (Matthew 1:19). Here is St. John Chrysostom's assessment:

Here, "just man" means adorned with every virtue. . . . Being a just man, that is, kind and self-controlled, Joseph wished to dismiss Mary quietly. Not only was he reluctant to punish her, but he would not even deliver her up. . . . You know how powerful a thing jealousy is. . . . But he was so free from this plague of the soul that he refused to inflict pain on the Virgin even in the slightest degree. . . . Do you perceive the moderation of this man? He did not chastise, he mentioned the affair to no one, . . . but he debated the matter with himself. . . . While he was pondering over all this, the angel appeared to him in sleep. And why not openly, as to the shepherds and to Zechariah? . . . Joseph was so ready to believe that he did not require such a manifestation. . . . He was ready to be easily led to good hope.

Chrysostom points out that Joseph demonstrates the same virtues when the angel appears again and commands him to head for Egypt right away (Matthew 2:13).

When Joseph heard this message, he was not offended, nor did he say, "Here indeed is something very puzzling! Didn't you just recently tell me, 'He will save his people'? And now he is unable to save himself, and we must flee on a long journey and change of place? This is contrary to your promise." No, he said nothing of the sort, for he was a man of faith. Nor did he inquire about the time of the return. . . . He obeyed and bent his will, bearing all his trials with joy.

Two Kinds of Searchers

Questions to Begin

15 minutes
Use a question or two to get warmed up for the reading.

---

1 What's the most awesome celestial spectacle you've ever seen?
❏ a comet
❏ a shooting star
❏ a planet or constellation
❏ the northern lights
❏ a solar or lunar eclipse
❏ other

---

2 How did your family approach Christmas gift giving when you were growing up? How do you approach it now?

---

3 Describe a "narrow escape" from some unpleasant or dangerous situation that you or someone close to you experienced.

5 minutes
*Read the passage aloud. Let individuals take turns reading
paragraphs.*

The Reading: Matthew 2:1–23

Follow That Star

[1] In the time of King Herod, after Jesus was born in Bethlehem of
Judea, wise men from the East came to Jerusalem, [2] asking, "Where is
the child who has been born king of the Jews? For we observed his
star at its rising, and have come to pay him homage." [3] When King
Herod heard this, he was frightened, and all Jerusalem with him;
[4] and calling together all the chief priests and scribes of the people, he
inquired of them where the Messiah was to be born. [5] They told him,
"In Bethlehem of Judea; for so it has been written by the prophet:

> [6] 'And you, Bethlehem, in the land of Judah,
>   are by no means least among the rulers of Judah;
> for from you shall come a ruler
>   who is to shepherd my people Israel.'"

[7] Then Herod secretly called for the wise men and learned from
them the exact time when the star had appeared. [8] Then he sent them
to Bethlehem, saying, "Go and search diligently for the child; and when
you have found him, bring me word so that I may also go and pay
him homage." [9] When they had heard the king, they set out; and there,
ahead of them, went the star that they had seen at its rising, until it
stopped over the place where the child was. [10] When they saw that the
star had stopped, they were overwhelmed with joy. [11] On entering the
house, they saw the child with Mary his mother; and they knelt down
and paid him homage. Then, opening their treasure chests, they
offered him gifts of gold, frankincense, and myrrh. [12] And having been
warned in a dream not to return to Herod, they left for their own
country by another road.

Flight and Fury

[13] Now after they had left, an angel of the Lord appeared to Joseph in
a dream and said, "Get up, take the child and his mother, and flee to
Egypt, and remain there until I tell you; for Herod is about to search
for the child, to destroy him." [14] Then Joseph got up, took the child
and his mother by night, and went to Egypt, [15] and remained there
until the death of Herod. This was to fulfill what had been spoken by
the Lord through the prophet, "Out of Egypt I have called my son."

16 When Herod saw that he had been tricked by the wise men, he was infuriated, and he sent and killed all the children in and around Bethlehem who were two years old or under, according to the time that he had learned from the wise men. 17 Then was fulfilled what had been spoken through the prophet Jeremiah:

18 "A voice was heard in Ramah,
     wailing and loud lamentation,
   Rachel weeping for her children;
     she refused to be consoled, because they are no
       more."

Going Home

19 When Herod died, an angel of the Lord suddenly appeared in a dream to Joseph in Egypt and said, 20 "Get up, take the child and his mother, and go to the land of Israel, for those who were seeking the child's life are dead." 21 Then Joseph got up, took the child and his mother, and went to the land of Israel. 22 But when he heard that Archelaus was ruling over Judea in place of his father Herod, he was afraid to go there. And after being warned in a dream, he went away to the district of Galilee. 23 There he made his home in a town called Nazareth, so that what had been spoken through the prophets might be fulfilled, "He will be called a Nazorean."

10 minutes
Choose questions according to your interest and time.

1 Reread Matthew 2:1–8. If you didn't already know the rest of the story, what impression of Herod would these verses give you?

2 How many wise men are there? Where is "the East" (Matthew 2:1)?

3 Herod and the wise men have opposing reactions to Jesus. Do you find their reactions surprising or not?

4 How does Matthew indicate that Jesus is a king? that his life will not be entirely peaceful?

5 Biblical writers rarely comment on their subjects' emotional states, but there are some strong emotions at work in this reading. Identify as many as you can.

6 Compare these two sets of verses: Matthew 2:13–15 and Matthew 2:20–21. What conclusions do you draw from your findings?

A Guide to the Reading

If participants have not read this section already, read it aloud. Otherwise go on to "Questions for Application."

Matthew explains Jesus' identity through a travel section featuring three divinely guided journeys. The first journey's destination is Bethlehem, to which a miraculous star guides "wise men from the East" (Matthew 2:1, 9–10). For the first time, we learn that this town, five miles south of Jerusalem, is where Jesus was born. This is crucial: Bethlehem was King David's ancestral home, and prophecies like the one quoted to Herod in Matthew 2:6 (Micah 5:2) specified that it would be the Messiah's birthplace too.

Egypt, the destination to which a second dream directs Joseph (Matthew 2:13), evokes his Old Testament namesake, another "dreamer" who went to Egypt and provided a safe haven for some of Jesus' ancestors (Genesis 37, 45). Especially, Egypt brings to mind Moses, who led the Israelites out of slavery to Pharaoh. This exodus is what the prophet Hosea described figuratively: "Out of Egypt I have called my son" (Matthew 2:15; Hosea 11:1). His words are fulfilled more literally in the return to the Promised Land of the Son, Jesus, who will lead God's people out of bondage to sin (Matthew 1:21).

Nazareth, the destination of the last divinely inspired journey, is a backwater town mentioned nowhere in the Old Testament. The allusion in Matthew 2:23 to the prophets' calling the Messiah a "Nazorean" may be a play on Hebrew words suggesting both the "branch" *(netser)* sprouting from David's family tree (Isaiah 11:1) and a person specially consecrated to God (a *nazir*—see Numbers 6:1–21).

The "wise men" are well named. They are magi— astrologers from Persia, Babylonia, or Arabia—whose study of nature has drawn them into a search for truth. Though ignorant of the Jewish Scriptures, they recognize Jesus' birth as a milestone calling for a serious investment of their time, effort, and money. They come prepared to celebrate, bearing three gifts (indicating *three* magi?) fit for a king. Early Christian writers called them kings, too, and found great symbolic meaning in their offerings: gold to honor royalty, incense to worship divinity, myrrh to show respect for a dead body prepared for burial.

The wise men's diligent seeking makes for ecstatic finding. Pointed toward Bethlehem by Herod's theological consultants, they thrill when the guiding star stops like an exclamation point over the right house. In a scene that is the centerpiece of this story, the Magi find "the child with Mary his mother" and pay him homage by falling prostrate (Matthew 2:2, 11). Matthew indicates that this is more than reverence for a king; it is adoration reserved for God, the type of worship the disciples will offer Jesus after his resurrection (28:9, 17).

If starlight shines on the Magi, a black cloud overshadows Herod. The Rome-appointed king of Judea is not rolling out the red carpet for a rival "king of the Jews" (Matthew 2:2). Though he has access to scriptural revelation and observes the Jewish law to some extent (with a no-pork diet), Herod cares about political power, not the promised Messiah. Moving from disquiet to sly malevolence, he plays devout in order to obtain information from the Magi. What he "learns"—in Greek, the word means finding out exactly—allows him to calculate his rival's age: already in 2:7, Herod is cold-bloodedly planning the murders executed in 2:16.

But the ruthless king is foiled. The Magi slip away quietly. An angelic dream warns Joseph of Herod's search-and-destroy operation (Matthew 2:12–13). Why don't other Bethlehem parents get an alert? Without raising the question, Matthew indicates that God has no part in Herod's bloody deed. Other events have happened "in order to fulfill" a prophecy (Matthew 1:22; 2:15, 23); in this case, prophecy is "fulfilled"—but without any notion of divine intent or purpose. Since at least the third century, the "Holy Innocents" who died in Jesus' place have been honored as the first martyrs for Christ.

This is a birth story with more weeping than singing. Its dark chords anticipate that religious and political authorities will again seek to "destroy" this "king of the Jews" (Matthew 2:2–4, 13; 27:1–2, 20, 37). Against this somber background, unassuming Joseph is a steady, reassuring presence whose actions speak more loudly than words. He shows us the secret of dealing well with good times and bad—utmost attentiveness to God's every word and utter faithfulness in obeying it.

Questions for Application

40 minutes
Choose questions according to your interest and time.

1 St. Gregory the Great said, "Herod symbolizes all those today who, falsely seeking after the Lord, never manage to find him." What are some of the reasons that might keep a person from truly seeking? What makes a search sincere?

2 How can an individual bring Christ to people who are seeking him—relatives, coworkers, friends, neighbors, and others? How can a parish be more welcoming to visitors and new parishioners?

3 Juan Maldonado, a sixteenth-century Jesuit scholar, said that God led the Magi to Christ through their study of the stars and that "in all things we can both seek and find God." Has God ever met you in unexpected places?

4 What could you do to meet people where they're at and help them in their seeking of God?

5 Refugees, immigrants, prisoners, students, nursing-home residents—the world is full of people far from home. What kinds of problems do they face? What could you or your parish do to help some of them?

6 Matthew does not report a single direct word of Joseph, which has the effect of highlighting his obedient actions. What lesson might there be for you in this?

7 For personal reflection: Homage was the wise men's most precious gift to Jesus. What gift do you think Jesus most wants from you right now?

One of the most important assets of a small group leader is his or her ability to listen.

Clarence and Edith Roberts, *Sharing of Scripture*

Approach to Prayer

15 minutes
Use this approach—or create your own!

◆ Ask someone to read aloud this reflection from St. Peter Chrysologus, a fifth-century bishop of Ravenna, Italy:

Today the magi gaze in deep wonder at what they see: heaven on earth, earth in heaven, man in God, God in man, one whom the whole universe cannot contain now enclosed in a tiny body. As they look, they believe and do not question, as their symbolic gifts bear witness: incense for God, gold for a king, myrrh for one who is to die.

Take a few minutes for silent reflection. Close with a short prayer, such as "Lord, we come to you as the Magi did, in wonder and thanksgiving. We adore and praise you. We offer ourselves to you." End with a Glory Be.

A Living Tradition

Remembering Rachel and Her Children

This section is a supplement for individual reading.

In a special way, the Bethlehem boys who were slaughtered at Herod's orders, victims of his paranoia and political ambitions (Matthew 2:16), have become patrons for many Christians active in pro-life work. "Holy Innocents" figures in the names of numerous outreaches to the unborn, their mothers, and all at-risk children. Catholics honor the Holy Innocents as martyrs and commemorate them on December 28. In many areas, their feast day is marked by prayer services, demonstrations, and Masses offered for pro-life concerns. Announcing one such Mass, Cardinal John O'Connor, the late archbishop of New York, said it was "in memory of all those innocents put to death at the direction of Herod, as well as the untold numbers slaughtered today by way of the horror of abortion."

"Holy Innocents" ministries remember abortion's "other victims" too—mothers, abortion providers, relatives and friends. The Church of the Holy Innocents—a New York City parish—features a shrine where Mass is celebrated once a month and people can stop in to pray at any time "in memory of the children who have died unborn." Many women grieving their abortions list their child's name in the "Book of Life" maintained at the shrine. Writing anonymously online, one woman who took advantage of their service said it made a significant contribution to her recovery.

Project Rachel is an especially well-known ministry that provides professional, one-on-one care to people struggling after an abortion. Founded in 1984 by Vicki Thorn, then director of Respect Life in the Archdiocese of Milwaukee, Project Rachel was inspired by the grief of a friend who had given up one baby for adoption and aborted another. "I can live with the adoption," said the friend. "I can't live with the abortion."

Project Rachel takes its name from Jeremiah 31:15, where Rachel, one of Israel's matriarchs, is pictured weeping as the ancient Israelites are marched into exile in Babylon. (Matthew applies her mourning to the children slain in Bethlehem—2:18.) Jeremiah's prophecy goes on to assure Rachel of future healing and restoration—which is also the vision of Project Rachel.

Gabriel on a Rescue Mission

Questions to Begin

15 minutes
Use a question or two to get warmed up for the reading.

1   What do you consider the most important day of your life?

2   Have you ever planned a big surprise for someone? Did you pull it off? How did they react?

3   Suppose you were given three wishes to make the world a better place. What would they be?

Read the passage aloud. Let individuals take turns reading paragraphs.

The Reading: Luke 1:5–38

Zechariah's Big Day

5 In the days of King Herod of Judea, there was a priest named Zechariah, who belonged to the priestly order of Abijah. His wife was a descendant of Aaron, and her name was Elizabeth. 6 Both of them were righteous before God, living blamelessly according to all the commandments and regulations of the Lord. 7 But they had no children, because Elizabeth was barren, and both were getting on in years.

8 Once when he was serving as priest before God and his section was on duty, 9 he was chosen by lot, according to the custom of the priesthood, to enter the sanctuary of the Lord and offer incense. 10 Now at the time of the incense offering, the whole assembly of the people was praying outside. 11 Then there appeared to him an angel of the Lord, standing at the right side of the altar of incense. 12 When Zechariah saw him, he was terrified; and fear overwhelmed him. 13 But the angel said to him, "Do not be afraid, Zechariah, for your prayer has been heard. Your wife Elizabeth will bear you a son, and you will name him John. 14 You will have joy and gladness, and many will rejoice at his birth, 15 for he will be great in the sight of the Lord. He must never drink wine or strong drink; even before his birth he will be filled with the Holy Spirit. 16 He will turn many of the people of Israel to the Lord their God. 17 With the spirit and power of Elijah he will go before him, to turn the hearts of parents to their children, and the disobedient to the wisdom of the righteous, to make ready a people prepared for the Lord."

A Sign with a Sting

18 Zechariah said to the angel, "How will I know that this is so? For I am an old man, and my wife is getting on in years." 19 The angel replied, "I am Gabriel. I stand in the presence of God, and I have been sent to speak to you and to bring you this good news. 20 But now, because you did not believe my words, which will be fulfilled in their time, you will become mute, unable to speak, until the day these things occur."

21 Meanwhile the people were waiting for Zechariah, and wondered at his delay in the sanctuary. 22 When he did come out, he could not speak to them, and they realized that he had seen a vision in the sanctuary. He kept motioning to them and remained unable to speak. 23 When his time of service was ended, he went to his home.

24 After those days his wife Elizabeth conceived, and for five months she remained in seclusion. She said, 25 "This is what the Lord has done for me when he looked favorably on me and took away the disgrace I have endured among my people."

Surprised by Joy

26 In the sixth month the angel Gabriel was sent by God to a town in Galilee called Nazareth, 27 to a virgin engaged to a man whose name was Joseph, of the house of David. The virgin's name was Mary. 28 And he came to her and said, "Greetings, favored one! The Lord is with you." 29 But she was much perplexed by his words and pondered what sort of greeting this might be. 30 The angel said to her, "Do not be afraid, Mary, for you have found favor with God. 31 And now, you will conceive in your womb and bear a son, and you will name him Jesus. 32 He will be great, and will be called the Son of the Most High, and the Lord God will give to him the throne of his ancestor David. 33 He will reign over the house of Jacob forever, and of his kingdom there will be no end." 34 Mary said to the angel, "How can this be, since I am a virgin?" 35 The angel said to her, "The Holy Spirit will come upon you, and the power of the Most High will overshadow you; therefore the child to be born will be holy; he will be called Son of God. 36 And now, your relative Elizabeth in her old age has also conceived a son; and this is the sixth month for her who was said to be barren. 37 For nothing will be impossible with God." 38 Then Mary said, "Here am I, the servant of the Lord; let it be with me according to your word." Then the angel departed from her.

10 minutes
Choose questions according to your interest and time.

1 Luke presents two couples. Of the four people, who has the most credentials? Who has the least?

2 What differences can you detect in how Gabriel relates to Zechariah and how he relates to Mary? in how they relate to him?

3 Gabriel gives Zechariah an assurance that his son will bring him great happiness (Luke 1:14). Does he give Mary a similar assurance?

4 In addition to the birth announcement, Gabriel has a sort of job description for each of the sons who are about to be conceived. Where are the assignments similar? Where are they different? Do they indicate which child will be greater?

5 What purposes are served by the sign that is given to Zechariah (Luke 1:20)?

6 Why do you think Elizabeth stays out of the public eye for the first five months of her pregnancy?

A Guide to the Reading

If participants have not read this section already, read it aloud. Otherwise go on to "Questions for Application."

In two separate episodes of one awesome story, a parent-to-be receives a surprise birth announcement for a son who is not yet conceived. Here begins Luke's account of the revelation of the astonishing "good news" of God's secret rescue plan for the whole human race (Luke 1:19; 2:10).

For Zechariah, it is already a red-letter day. As a member of the "order of Abijah" (Luke 1:5), one of the twenty-four divisions of Israel's eighteen thousand priests, he has given two weeks' annual service at the Jerusalem temple all his adult life. Now in his autumn years, he has finally been selected for the one-time honor of officiating at an incense offering. Scene one opens with Zechariah standing at the incense altar within the temple sanctuary. It is a solemn moment: he is as close to the sacred inner chamber, the Holy of holies, as anyone but the high priest can ever get.

Whatever Zechariah's hopes for this mountaintop experience, he is blown away by Gabriel (who is no cute cherub—see Daniel 8:17) and the angel's news of an answer to prayer (Luke 1:13). But which prayer? Certainly, Zechariah has asked God for a child. But if this is the evening incense service, as seems likely, he and the people (Luke 1:10) are offering the prescribed prayers for Israel's salvation.

As it turns out, this is a two-for-one answer to prayer. Israel will rejoice at John's birth, for he will be a great and Spirit-filled prophet who turns many hearts back to God (Luke 1:14–17). And Zechariah and Elizabeth will "have joy and gladness," the stigma of their childlessness erased (Luke 1:14, 25). No longer will the blameless couple be suspected as being unworthy of God's blessing ("No children, eh? Must be a secret sin . . ."). Like a new Abraham and Sarah (Genesis 21:1), they are vindicated by the delightful surprise of this late-in-life pregnancy.

Some five or six months later, Gabriel takes another person by surprise. The setting is an unimpressive hamlet (see John 1:46) some eighty miles north of Jerusalem. The recipient, a teenage girl with no apparent social clout, is presumably going about a routine day of humble activities—grinding barley, milking the family goat, drawing water. If she has any outstanding prayer requests, we are not told about them. In fact, Luke offers more information about this young woman's fiancé than about her (1:27).

Mary's hidden grace is unveiled when the majestic messenger hails her almost deferentially as one uniquely "favored" by the Lord (Luke 1:28, 30). He follows up with a declaration of God's presence that implies a special mission (compare with Judges 6:12). A reflective person, Mary is more "perplexed" by this exalted greeting than frightened at the sight of Gabriel (Luke 1:29).

In the angel's declaration, Mary finds some answers, along with mysteries to ponder for a lifetime. Awesome but easiest to grasp is the news that Israel's waiting is over: her Son will be the Son of David, the Messiah (Luke 1:32–33; 2 Samuel 7:9, 13–14, 16). Absolutely staggering is the revelation that Jesus is also the "Son of God" (Luke 1:35). If John is the first ray of light heralding God's new mercy, Jesus will be the high noon of God's face-to-face presence. Luke underlines Jesus' unique relationship with God by calling attention to Mary's virginity and her miraculous conception of Jesus by the Holy Spirit (1:27, 34–35).

Apparently with some distrust, Zechariah asked for confirmation of Gabriel's promise (Luke 1:18, 20). His "How will I know?" got him a punitive sign: nine months of silence in which to contemplate Elizabeth's swelling silhouette (Luke 1:22). Mary meets a greater test of faith with a pensive but not unbelieving "How?" (Luke 1:34). Although she has not asked for a sign, she receives one: the news of Elizabeth's pregnancy, which has been kept under wraps (Luke 1:24).

Mary does not need to go off and pray at length about how to respond. With more to lose than Zechariah and less assurance that things will turn out well for her personally, she accepts the risks of surrendering to God's plan. Gabriel's assertion that "nothing"— literally, in the Greek, "no word"—"will be impossible with God" (Luke 1:37; see Genesis 18:14) is probably not a new idea for Mary, but her response echoes his phrasing. She gives God's "word" free play in her life, and thus "the Word became flesh and lived among us" (Luke 1:38; John 1:14).

Questions for Application

40 minutes
Choose questions according to your interest and time.

---

1 In what area of your life do you need encouragement to keep on praying for something? Is there anything in today's reading that could help you "to pray always and not to lose heart" (Luke 18:1)?

---

2 Has it ever seemed to you that God was inviting you to do something you felt unequipped for? How did you respond? What was the result?

---

3 When it comes to following Jesus, where do you fall on the scale between "supercautious" and "risk taker"? When is it prudent to take risks in faith?

---

4 Instead of being filled with wine or strong drink, from which he is to abstain, John will be filled with the Holy Spirit (Luke 1:15). Though his is a special vocation, what does it suggest about the value of occasional fasting and other penitential measures? (See also Ephesians 5:18.) How should you make use of these disciplines?

5 Is it ever acceptable to ask for a sign from God? What are the possible dangers?

6 Gabriel announces good news to both Zechariah and Mary, but only in Mary's case does he wait for a sign of consent (Luke 1:38). What does each scenario reveal about God's dealings with individuals?

7 For personal reflection: Mary expresses that she belongs fully to God by calling herself his servant—literally, in the Greek, his "slave" (Luke 1:38). Would that description fit you, or are you serving more than one master?

Don't try to control what the Bible is allowed to say to you, and don't hold back your spontaneous responses and questions.

H. A. Nielsen, *The Bible—As If for the First Time*

Approach to Prayer

15 minutes
Use this approach—or create your own!

♦ Express your thanks for Mary's yes and Jesus' birth by praying the Angelus, with one person praying the A parts and everyone praying the B parts:

A. The angel of the Lord declared unto Mary.

B. And she conceived of the Holy Spirit.
   Hail Mary.

A. Behold the handmaid of the Lord.

B. May it be done unto me according to your word.
   Hail Mary.

A. And the Word was made flesh,

B. And dwelled among us.
   Hail Mary.

A. Pray for us, O holy Mother of God.

B. That we may be made worthy of the promises of Christ.

A. Pour forth, we beseech you, O Lord, your grace into our hearts, that we, to whom the Incarnation of Christ, your Son, was made known by the message of an angel, may be brought by his Passion and cross to the glory of his Resurrection.

B. Amen.

Saints in the Making

Angels in Our Darkest Nights

This section is a supplement for individual reading.

The German Jesuit Alfred Delp endured seven months in a Nazi prison before his execution for "high treason" in February 1945. This is one of many meditations he wrote there.

Never have I entered on Advent so vitally and intensely alert as I am now. When I pace my cell, up and down, three paces one way and three the other, my hands manacled, an unknown fate in front of me, then the tidings of our Lord's coming to redeem the world and deliver it have a different and much more vivid meaning. And my mind keeps going back to the angel someone gave me as a present during Advent two or three years ago. It bore the inscription: "Be of good cheer. The Lord is near." A bomb destroyed it. The same bomb killed the donor, and I often have the feeling that he is rendering me some heavenly aid. It would be impossible to endure the horror of these days . . . if there were not this other knowledge . . . of the promises that have been given and fulfilled. And the awareness of the angels of good tidings, uttering their blessed messages in the midst of all this trouble and sowing seed of blessing where it will sprout in the middle of the night. Then angels of Advent are not the bright jubilant beings who trumpet the tidings of fulfillment to a waiting world. Quiet and unseen they enter our shabby rooms and our hearts as they did of old. In the silence of the night they pose God's questions and proclaim the wonders of him with whom all things are possible. . . .

May the time never come when mankind no longer hears the soft footsteps of the herald angel or his cheering words that penetrate the soul. Should such a time come, all will be lost. . . . For the first thing man must do if he wants to raise himself out of this sterile life is to open his heart to the golden seed which God's angels are waiting to sow in it. And one other thing: he must himself throughout these grey days go forth as a bringer of good tidings. There is so much despair that cries out for comfort. . . . God's messengers, who have themselves reaped the fruits of divine seeds sown even in the darkest hours, know how to wait for the fullness of harvest.

SONGS OF PRAISE

Questions to Begin

15 minutes
Use a question or two to get warmed up for the reading.

1 What's the most surprising invitation you've ever received?

2 What kind of message would you just love to receive today?
- ❑ a greeting card (preferably with a check enclosed)
- ❑ a warm greeting from someone who's been cool to you lately
- ❑ an e-mail from a friend who has been out of touch
- ❑ a thank-you note
- ❑ a notice that something is going to be done or delivered on schedule
- ❑ a bouquet or box of chocolates
- ❑ other

5 minutes
Read the passage aloud. Let individuals take turns reading
paragraphs.

The Reading: Luke 1:39–79

Time to Celebrate!

[39] In those days Mary set out and went with haste to a Judean town
in the hill country, [40] where she entered the house of Zechariah and
greeted Elizabeth. [41] When Elizabeth heard Mary's greeting, the child
leaped in her womb. And Elizabeth was filled with the Holy Spirit
[42] and exclaimed with a loud cry, "Blessed are you among women,
and blessed is the fruit of your womb. [43] And why has this happened
to me, that the mother of my Lord comes to me? [44] For as soon as I
heard the sound of your greeting, the child in my womb leaped for
joy. [45] And blessed is she who believed that there would be a
fulfillment of what was spoken to her by the Lord."

Why Mary Rejoices

[46] And Mary said,
> "My soul magnifies the Lord,
> [47] and my spirit rejoices in God my Savior,
> [48] for he has looked with favor on the lowliness of his
> servant.
> Surely, from now on all generations will call
> me blessed;
> [49] for the Mighty One has done great things for me,
> and holy is his name.
> [50] His mercy is for those who fear him
> from generation to generation.
> [51] He has shown strength with his arm;
> he has scattered the proud in the thoughts of their
> hearts.
> [52] He has brought down the powerful from their thrones,
> and lifted up the lowly;
> [53] he has filled the hungry with good things,
> and sent the rich away empty.
> [54] He has helped his servant Israel,
> in remembrance of his mercy,
> [55] according to the promise he made to our ancestors,
> to Abraham and to his descendants forever."

[56] And Mary remained with her about three months and then
returned to her home.

⁵⁷ Now the time came for Elizabeth to give birth, and she bore a son. ⁵⁸ Her neighbors and relatives heard that the Lord had shown his great mercy to her, and they rejoiced with her.

⁵⁹ On the eighth day they came to circumcise the child, and they were going to name him Zechariah after his father. ⁶⁰ But his mother said, "No; he is to be called John." . . . ⁶² Then they began motioning to his father to find out what name he wanted to give him. ⁶³ He asked for a writing tablet and wrote, "His name is John." And all of them were amazed. ⁶⁴ Immediately his mouth was opened and his tongue freed, and he began to speak, praising God. ⁶⁵ Fear came over all their neighbors, and all these things were talked about throughout the entire hill country of Judea. . . .

⁶⁷ Then his father Zechariah was filled with the Holy Spirit and spoke this prophecy:

⁶⁸ "Blessed be the Lord God of Israel,
      for he has looked favorably on his people and
            redeemed them.
⁶⁹ He has raised up a mighty savior for us
      in the house of his servant David,
⁷⁰ as he spoke through the mouth of his holy prophets
            from of old. . . .
⁷² Thus he has shown the mercy promised to our ancestors,
      and has remembered his holy covenant,
⁷³ the oath that he swore to our ancestor Abraham,
      to grant us ⁷⁴ that we, being rescued from the hands
            of our enemies,
      might serve him without fear, ⁷⁵ in holiness and
            righteousness
      before him all our days.
⁷⁶ And you, child, will be called the prophet of the
            Most High;
      for you will go before the Lord to prepare his ways,
⁷⁷ to give knowledge of salvation to his people
      by the forgiveness of their sins.
⁷⁸ By the tender mercy of our God,
      the dawn from on high will break upon us,
⁷⁹ to give light to those who sit in darkness and in the
            shadow of death,
      to guide our feet into the way of peace."

Questions for Careful Reading

10 minutes
Choose questions according to your interest and time.

1 Why do you suppose Mary is in such a rush to see Elizabeth (Luke 1:39)?

2 In their prayers, both Mary and Zechariah praise God for doing certain things. Make a list of Mary's reasons for praise, then of Zechariah's. How do the two compare? What picture of God emerges?

3 The Holy Spirit is the invisible actor in this drama of salvation. What sorts of things does he do? (Look back to Luke 1:15 and 1:35.)

4 According to Luke 1:50, 1:72, and 1:78, what seems to be God's fundamental attitude toward the world? How would you describe the particular characteristic that is being highlighted?

5 What does "fear" mean in Luke 1:65? in 1:74?

A Guide to the Reading

If participants have not read this section already, read it aloud. Otherwise go on to "Questions for Application."

Just in case anybody was wondering whether Mary said yes to God out of a mere sense of duty, her "haste" (Luke 1:39) in making an arduous four-day journey signals quite the opposite. Enthusiasm is in the air as she travels to see Elizabeth, whose miraculous pregnancy makes her the perfect confidante and prayer partner for celebrating God's greatness. Before Mary has a chance to disclose her own astounding news, however, a sudden intervention of the Holy Spirit makes explanations superfluous.

Mary has already received the Holy Spirit and conceived Jesus by his power (Luke 1:35). Now the Spirit falls on John, who begins heralding the Lord's way with a joyful leap of recognition that triggers his own mother's reception of the Spirit (Luke 1:15, 17, 41, 44, 76). Rather amusingly, St. Bernard of Clairvaux likens the unborn John to a lighted candle that suddenly illumines the bushel basket under which it is hidden. Indeed, Elizabeth is enlightened to an astonishing degree. In a flash, she recognizes the source of Mary's pregnancy and favored status, even acknowledging Jesus as "my Lord" (Luke 1:42–43). She identifies the reasons for honoring Mary—not only her physical motherhood of the Messiah but also her faith (Luke 1:42, 45). As Elizabeth exclaims "blessed is she," she turns out of Luke's story to face us directly, inviting us to join with her in praise of Mary, the first and best of Jesus' disciples.

Mary's exuberant outpouring of praise in declaration of God's mercy to her (Luke 1:46–50) and to his people (1:51–55) contrasts sharply with the silence of Zechariah, whose lips have been sealed by unbelief (1:20). "Faith is thus a condition for speaking God's life-giving word," comments New Testament scholar Eugene LaVerdiere, S.S.S. What about us? Does our own lack of faith make us mute in situations where we should speak out? Do our pious words sometimes ring hollow because we do not fully believe what we profess?

Sidelined for the duration of Elizabeth's pregnancy, Zechariah regains his place of honor through an act of obedience. Neighbors and relatives who may have been calling his seven-day-old son "little Zack" are amazed when Zechariah insists that the name is nonnegotiable and is, in fact, a done deal: "His name *is* John" (Luke 1:13, 63; emphasis added). Zechariah has barely finished carving *John* into the wax-covered writing tablet when he, too, is filled with the Spirit and bursts out with pent-up praise (Luke 1:64).

Zechariah's Spirit-inspired words, like Mary's, are a time-out from the action. They interpret the meaning and significance of the events that have occurred, stimulating us to better appreciate the impact of Jesus' coming for ourselves and celebrate it. Each canticle, as the two speeches are traditionally called, is a mosaic of biblical texts and themes that connect God's *now* activity with his saving actions in the past. What God has done for Mary and Zechariah is part of an ongoing story of mercy that began with Abraham, has unfolded "from generation to generation," and now takes a startling new turn as it reaches down to us (Luke 1:50, 55, 72–73, 79). With the Incarnation, divine mercy is revealed in a human face.

In prophetic words spoken directly to baby John, Zechariah foresees the child's mission as the servant of the coming Lord, who will save his people from their sins (Luke 1:76–77). Picture this newly vocal father exulting aloud as he holds his infant son. By his very act of proclaiming God's greatness, he is demonstrating *why* we are saved from our sins and our enemies: so that we can serve and worship God "without fear, in holiness and righteousness before him all our days" (Luke 1:74–75).

It is the joy and not the cost of serving God that predominates in this story of two wondrous births. Yet even in Mary's celebration of God's astounding reversals—his choice of the lowly over the proud, powerful, and rich (Luke 1:48, 51–53)—there is a hint of the cross. Her canticle proclaims "that wealth and power are not real values at all, since they have no standing in God's sight," says New Testament scholar Raymond Brown. "This is not an easy message."

Rejoicing friends and relatives undoubtedly foresaw a rosy future for these two sons who arrived surrounded by such amazing signs (Luke 1:65–66; 2:18, 33). Who among them could have guessed that for presenting true values and a challenging message, John and Jesus would pay with their lives?

Questions for Application

40 minutes
Choose questions according to your interest and time.

1 Elizabeth rejoices whole-heartedly in what God has done for Mary. Do you generally respond this way to someone else's good news, or do you struggle with envy and resentment? As a member of the Church, how can you grow in the kind of solidarity that St. Paul talks about: "If one member suffers, all suffer together with it; if one member is honored, all rejoice together with it" (1 Corinthians 12:26)?

2 False humility wants to downplay or deny the "great things" God does in and through us (Luke 1:49). True humility, as Mary displays it, involves accurate self-assessment (Romans 12:3), leading to praise of God. Does your idea of humility need any readjusting? How can you align it with Mary's?

3 How does Mary experience God's mercy? How do Zechariah and Elizabeth experience it? What do their experiences reveal about the mercy God wishes to extend to you? to the world?

4 New Testament scholar Joseph Fitzmyer, S.J., says that Luke 1:48 "implies a respect" for Mary as both Jesus' mother and his first and best follower and that it "expresses a fundamental attitude of all Christians toward the believing Mother of the Lord." Do you share this attitude? How could you get to know Mary better?

5 Over the course of your life, who have been the messengers sent to smooth your way to God? How have you received them? For whom is God calling you to perform the same service?

6 How does the way you live contribute to the purpose for which Jesus came: to create a people who serve God "without fear, in holiness and righteousness before him" (Luke 1:74–75)? What life change does this reading lead you to consider?

How can we read the Bible so as to hear the sound of Christ's voice? We need silence for this, because amidst the flood of words and noise that forces itself on us, the voice of Christ is quite soft.

The Taizé Community, *Listening with the Heart*

Approach to Prayer

15 minutes
Use this approach—or create your own!

♦ The canticles of Mary (Luke 1:46–55) and Zechariah (Luke 1:68–79) hold a special place in the Liturgy of the Hours, the official prayer of the Church, which is recited throughout the day. Often called the Benedictus and the Magnificat (Latin for their opening words, *Blessed* and *It praises*), the canticles are said daily—Zechariah's at Morning Prayer, Mary's at Evening. (Night Prayer in the Church's Liturgy of the Hours features Simeon's canticle, the "Nunc Dimittis"—Latin for its first words: *Now you are dismissing*—Luke 2:29–32).

Together, pray Mary's or Zechariah's canticle in thanksgiving for the "great things" God has done and continues to do. Pray responsorially if you wish, dividing up into two groups that read alternate lines aloud.

A Living Tradition

When Jesus Comes to Visit

This section is a supplement for individual reading.

St. Francis de Sales often meditated on Luke's account of Mary's visit to her relative Elizabeth. Taking it as a given that Joseph accompanied her and that the trip was an errand of mercy to help Elizabeth, he liked to picture the couple en route to Zechariah's house in "a Judean town in the hill country" (Luke 1:39). "I should love to know something about the conversation of these two great souls," St. Francis admitted. He speculated that Mary was so attuned and Joseph so attentive to the Child she was carrying that the two were united in a "love beyond measure" that radiated outward like an especially fragrant perfume. "I am entirely preoccupied by this dear Visitation!" he wrote.

In 1610, together with St. Jane de Chantal, Francis founded the Visitation of Holy Mary, a religious order of women whose life was to combine charity toward neighbor and the inner focus on God exemplified by Mary in her visit to Elizabeth. Given the climate of seventeenth-century religious life, says Thomas Daily, O.S.F.S., the new order was "a unique approach." First, the Visitation "would welcome any woman who was drawn to follow the natural inclination of her heart toward union with God in prayer, and especially those who, for physical or emotional reasons, would not be accepted in other congregations. Second, the members of this religious institute, unlike other monasteries of the time, would not be strictly cloistered. As a result of the interior union of their own heart with God and as a way of demonstrating the supreme virtue of charity, these sisters would go out into the town to serve the poor and sick."

As things turned out, Church authorities required Francis and Jane to transform the Visitation into a cloistered community. Nonetheless, the Visitation order maintained its foundational vision of a God who comes to meet his people and take up loving residence in their heart. "In many ways, Salesian spirituality is one of Jesus coming to our homes—to where we live, work, play, and pray," observes Joseph F. Power, O.S.F.S.

Quite literally, this is what Jesus did in the first visitation of all, in first-century Judea.

Away in a Manger

Questions to Begin

15 minutes
Use a question or two to get warmed up for the reading.

1   Write down the titles of your
two favorite Christmas carols;
then compare your answers
with those of the people in your
group. Is there a consensus?
(For individuals: Sing your
favorite Christmas carol—or
sing along with it on CD or
tape—as a way to get in the
mood for today's reading.)

2   Describe the most unusual
Nativity scene you've ever seen.

3   What's the most uncomfortable
trip you've ever taken?

5 minutes
Read the passage aloud. Let individuals take turns reading
paragraphs.

The Reading: Luke 2:1–21

O Little Town of Bethlehem

[1] In those days a decree went out from Emperor Augustus that all the
world should be registered. [2] This was the first registration and was
taken while Quirinius was governor of Syria. [3] All went to their own
towns to be registered. [4] Joseph also went from the town of Nazareth
in Galilee to Judea, to the city of David called Bethlehem, because
he was descended from the house and family of David. [5] He went
to be registered with Mary, to whom he was engaged and who was
expecting a child. [6] While they were there, the time came for her
to deliver her child. [7] And she gave birth to her firstborn son and
wrapped him in bands of cloth, and laid him in a manger, because
there was no place for them in the inn.

Angels We Have Heard on High

[8] In that region there were shepherds living in the fields, keeping
watch over their flock by night. [9] Then an angel of the Lord stood
before them, and the glory of the Lord shone around them, and they
were terrified. [10] But the angel said to them, "Do not be afraid; for
see—I am bringing you good news of great joy for all the people:
[11] to you is born this day in the city of David a Savior, who is the
Messiah, the Lord. [12] This will be a sign for you: you will find a
child wrapped in bands of cloth and lying in a manger." [13] And
suddenly there was with the angel a multitude of the heavenly host,
praising God and saying,

> [14] "Glory to God in the highest heaven,
>   and on earth peace among those whom he favors!"

Come, All Ye Faithful

[15] When the angels had left them and gone into heaven, the shepherds
said to one another, "Let us go now to Bethlehem and see this thing
that has taken place, which the Lord has made known to us." [16] So
they went with haste and found Mary and Joseph, and the child lying
in the manger. [17] When they saw this, they made known what had
been told them about this child; [18] and all who heard it were amazed

at what the shepherds told them. 19 But Mary treasured all these words and pondered them in her heart. 20 The shepherds returned, glorifying and praising God for all they had heard and seen, as it had been told them.

21 After eight days had passed, it was time to circumcise the child; and he was called Jesus, the name given by the angel before he was conceived in the womb.

10 minutes
Choose questions according to your interest and time.

1 In what ways does Luke set up a contrast between human and divine power and majesty in today's reading?

2 We often imagine that a hardhearted innkeeper turned Mary and Joseph away. But the Greek word translated "inn" in Luke 2:7 is a general term for any place of hospitality, including a guest room in a house. If the end of 2:7 was translated "no space in the guest room," what scenarios might this verse suggest?

3 What details are emphasized in Luke's description of the setting of Jesus' birth? Does the description match your Christmas manger scene?

4 Who is "you" in Luke 2:10 and 2:11?

5 What kind of peace does Luke 2:14 refer to? What is its source?

6 Mary praised God for exalting the lowly over the powerful (Luke 1:48, 51–53). How are the lowly lifted up in today's reading?

A Guide to the Reading

If participants have not read this section already, read it aloud. Otherwise go on to "Questions for Application."

In those days" (Luke 2:1), the one who was hailed with titles like "son of a god" and "savior" was Emperor Augustus. Grandnephew and adopted heir of Julius Caesar, Augustus headed the seemingly invincible Roman Empire. He could set "all the world" moving with one word of command—like the census decree that sends his subjects scurrying off to be counted in "their own towns" (Luke 2:1, 3). Law-abiding Joseph complies and takes Mary along on the eighty-five-mile trip from Nazareth to Bethlehem, where his ancestor David lived twenty-eight generations before.

For Jews, the census was a disturbing reminder of their political powerlessness. But things are not always as they appear. Without realizing it, the Roman emperor, the most powerful person in the world, is serving God's plan. His edict ensures that Jesus will be born in Bethlehem, in fulfillment of prophecy. Augustus may be the most impressive mover and shaker on the international scene, but he himself is an unwitting agent in the hands of the Prime Mover. (Something to remember as we watch the evening news.)

Furthermore, mighty Augustus is out of the most privileged information loop. The celestial proclamation of "good news of great joy for all the people" (Luke 2:10) comes to shepherds, night workers on a low rung of the social ladder. The titles the angel uses—Savior, Messiah, and Lord (Luke 2:11)—herald not a little caesar whose decrees and empire will ultimately vanish, but the King of kings, who brings true, lasting peace (Luke 2:14).

The splendor of the angelic sound-and-light show contrasts with the humble sign given to the shepherds: "a child wrapped in bands of cloth and lying in a manger" (Luke 2:7, 12, 16). Luke stresses the two details. The "bands of cloth" are to keep Jesus' limbs straight, according to the custom of the time. They suggest his solidarity with the people he has come to save and perhaps also his kingly status, by association with Solomon: this richest of Israel's kings "was nursed with care in swaddling cloths" (Wisdom 7:4). No less royal is Mary's loving welcome of her "firstborn" (Luke 2:7). The Greek word does not necessarily mean "first of many"; here it emphasizes that Jesus has the status given firstborn sons by the Mosaic law.

The second stressed detail is Jesus' crib: a manger, or animal feeding trough (Luke 2:7, 12, 16). Justin, the second-century Church Father who grew up in Palestine, spoke of the manger being in a cave. Perhaps he was referring to the fact that many houses in the area had a back room built into the side of a hill—a "cave" in which people sheltered their sheep and goats when the weather was bad. Other commentators pictured the manger in a barn or open-air feeding area. Early and modern writers have seen the manger as a symbolic expression of God's reproach, reflecting Isaiah 1:3: "The ox knows its owner, and the donkey its master's crib; but Israel does not know [me], my people do not understand."

Jesus does not come into the world with the panoply of a VIP. As the early English commentator Bede wrote: "It should be carefully noted that the sign . . . is not a child enfolded in Tyrian purple [dyed purple cloth was terrifically expensive, a badge of wealth and power] but one wrapped round with rough pieces of cloth; he is not to be found in an ornate golden bed, but in a manger." But at least some of the people who appear in the Nativity story recognize it as great good news. Luke 2:15–20 presents one neutral and two positive responses. What can we learn from them?

The shepherds model simple trust. They believe in the sign, seek it eagerly, and give testimony when they find it. The first evangelists in Luke's Gospel, the shepherds encourage us to go "glorifying and praising God" for all that we ourselves have "heard and seen" of his great mercy (Luke 2:20).

The neutral response comes from those who hear the shepherds' report. Like the neighbors and relatives at John's naming party, they are "amazed" (Luke 1:63; 2:18). Amazement is an appropriate reaction to the supernatural, but it is not faith. How often in Jesus' life will onlookers be astonished by his words and actions without following through to an accurate conclusion (Luke 4:22; 20:26)?

Mary, who is as amazed as anyone else, retains and reflects on these marvelous events and keeps trying to hit on their correct meaning (Luke 1:29; 2:19; see also 2:51). Secure in her understanding of God's love and faithfulness, she can live with a few question marks. At the same time, she presses on to a deeper knowledge of this new thing that God is doing.

Questions for Application

40 minutes
Choose questions according to your interest and time.

1 Jesus is born in a humble setting, and his coming goes unnoticed by most of the world. Can you detect humble ways in which he is being born today in your life? in the lives of people you know? in the world? How can you nurture and encourage these new births?

2 The angel's song (Luke 2:14) forms the opening words of the Gloria in the Mass. Why are these words an appropriate expression of gratefulness for the gift of Jesus in the Eucharist? What could you do to grow in understanding and appreciation of so great a gift?

3 The angels and shepherds praise God. Is praise a part of your prayer? How could you make praising God a higher priority?

4 The shepherds go and tell about what they have seen and heard. In what ways do you let the people you live and work with know about what God has done for you and for the world? What more could you do?

5 God works faithfully in the midst of human events, even when appearances seem to deny his presence or power. Are there situations in your life where you find this especially hard to believe? Does anything in today's reading help you understand these situations better?

6 Jesus' last greeting to his disciples in Luke's Gospel—"Peace be with you"—recalls the angel choir's "on earth peace" (24:36; 2:14). What is God's peace? How can we pursue "the way of peace" (Luke 1:79) and help others to walk it too?

How can we read the Bible so as to hear the sound of Christ's voice? We need . . . to share, to communicate what we have heard and to listen to what others have understood. Nobody can grasp, all by themselves, all the fullness of Christ.

The Taizé Community, *Listening with the Heart*

Approach to Prayer

15 minutes
Use this approach—or create your own!

♦ Have someone in the group read aloud this prayer by St. Catherine of Siena:

O depth of love! What heart could keep from breaking at the sight of your greatness descending to the lowliness of our humanity? We are your image, and now by making yourself one with us, you have become our humanity, veiling your eternal divinity. . . . And why? For love! You, God, became human and we have been made divine!

After a few moments' silent reflection, end by singing a Christmas carol. If you reached a consensus during the "Questions to Begin" section, sing that favorite carol. Otherwise, choose one that everyone in the group knows.

Saints in the Making

The First Noel

This section is a supplement for individual reading.

On Christmas Eve 1925, Bertha Spafford Vester was hurrying to sing Christmas carols at the Shepherds' Fields, near Bethlehem. American born, she had lived in Jerusalem since she was three. Her parents had moved there from Chicago in 1881 after a staggering series of personal tragedies. With a small group of friends, they bought a house just inside the walls of Jerusalem's Old City. Taking literally the words of Jesus in Matthew 25:35, the little community opened their doors to everyone in need.

Bertha had barely left the house that day when she encountered a weary-looking couple. The woman was clearly ill and held a small bundle.

I stopped and asked where they were going. The man answered, "Allah knows." I peeked into the bundle and found it contained a wee baby only a few days old. I said, "Your wife is very sick." "I know it," he replied. "I brought her for six hours on donkey-back to the hospital, only to find it closed . . ." I was greatly touched. I thought as I stood beside the mother and child that I was rushing off to sing carols in the shepherds' fields and to commemorate the birth of a babe who was born in a stable and placed in a manger because there was no room in the inn, and here before me stood a rustic Madonna and babe, and, metaphorically speaking, no room for them in the inn.

The woman got a hospital bed, with Bertha's help, but died during the night. "If I take my baby boy to my cave home, he will die," her husband told Bertha, begging that she take the child. "How could I refuse? Certainly these poor people had come up the hill, trusting that Allah would help them, and Allah must not fail them."

Within a week, Noel, as they named the infant, had been joined by two more babies. So began the "Baby Home" that developed into the Spafford Children's Center. Today, it provides health-care services for more than three thousand children a year.

Before her death in 1968, just after turning ninety, Bertha Spafford Vester explained the secret of the center's survival in Jerusalem's turbulent political climate: "We got along well with everyone, because they knew we were not serving them but God."

DIVINE APPOINTMENTS IN THE TEMPLE

Questions to Begin

15 minutes
Use a question or two to get warmed up for the reading.

1 What's the most valuable thing you've ever lost? Did you find it?

2 Have you ever experienced a remarkable coincidence that seemed as though it had been divinely orchestrated?

3 When you were growing up, was there any elderly person who played a significant role in your life?

5 minutes
*Read the passage aloud. Let individuals take turns reading
paragraphs.*

The Reading: Luke 2:22–52

Blessing and Warning

22 When the time came for their purification according to the law of
Moses, they brought him up to Jerusalem to present him to the Lord
23 (as it is written in the law of the Lord, "Every firstborn male shall
be designated as holy to the Lord"), 24 and they offered a sacrifice
according to what is stated in the law of the Lord, "a pair of turtle-
doves or two young pigeons."

25 Now there was a man in Jerusalem whose name was Simeon;
this man was righteous and devout, looking forward to the consolation of Israel, and the Holy Spirit rested on him. 26 It had been
revealed to him by the Holy Spirit that he would not see death before
he had seen the Lord's Messiah. 27 Guided by the Spirit, Simeon came
into the temple; and when the parents brought in the child Jesus, to
do for him what was customary under the law, 28 Simeon took him in
his arms and praised God, saying,

29 "Master, now you are dismissing your servant in peace,
according to your word;
30 for my eyes have seen your salvation,
31 which you have prepared in the presence of all
peoples,
32 a light for revelation to the Gentiles
and for glory to your people Israel."

33 And the child's father and mother were amazed at what was
being said about him. 34 Then Simeon blessed them and said to his
mother Mary, "This child is destined for the falling and the rising of
many in Israel, and to be a sign that will be opposed 35 so that the
inner thoughts of many will be revealed—and a sword will pierce
your own soul too."

36 There was also a prophet, Anna the daughter of Phanuel, of
the tribe of Asher. She was of a great age, having lived with her
husband seven years after her marriage, 37 then as a widow to the age
of eighty-four. She never left the temple but worshiped there with
fasting and prayer night and day. 38 At that moment she came, and
began to praise God and to speak about the child to all who were
looking for the redemption of Jerusalem.

³⁹ When they had finished everything required by the law of the Lord, they returned to Galilee, to their own town of Nazareth. ⁴⁰ The child grew and became strong, filled with wisdom; and the favor of God was upon him.

Lost and Found in God's House

⁴¹ Now every year his parents went to Jerusalem for the festival of the Passover. ⁴² And when he was twelve years old, they went up as usual for the festival. ⁴³ When the festival was ended and they started to return, the boy Jesus stayed behind in Jerusalem, but his parents did not know it. ⁴⁴ Assuming that he was in the group of travelers, they went a day's journey. Then they started to look for him among their relatives and friends. ⁴⁵ When they did not find him, they returned to Jerusalem to search for him. ⁴⁶ After three days they found him in the temple, sitting among the teachers, listening to them and asking them questions. ⁴⁷ And all who heard him were amazed at his understanding and his answers. ⁴⁸ When his parents saw him they were astonished; and his mother said to him, "Child, why have you treated us like this? Look, your father and I have been searching for you in great anxiety." ⁴⁹ He said to them, "Why were you searching for me? Did you not know that I must be in my Father's house?" ⁵⁰ But they did not understand what he said to them. ⁵¹ Then he went down with them and came to Nazareth, and was obedient to them. His mother treasured all these things in her heart.

⁵² And Jesus increased in wisdom and in years, and in divine and human favor.

10 minutes
Choose questions according to your interest and time.

1 In what ways do Simeon and Anna resemble Zechariah and Elizabeth? What characteristics identify them as credible witnesses to Jesus?

2 Where do you find evidence that people in today's reading are obedient to the Mosaic law? sensitive to the activity of the Holy Spirit?

3 What is it about Jesus that amazes the people in the temple? that amazes Mary and Joseph in Luke 2:33? in 2:48?

4 For what does Simeon thank God? What trouble does he foresee for Jesus? Why does he address the warning to Mary alone?

5 What picture of the holy family's relationships do you get from Mary's words to Jesus in Luke 2:48?

6 Compare Luke 2:22 and 2:41–42 with 2:51. Who is the subject of the "traveling" verbs in each verse? Where does the shift in subjects occur? Is the change significant?

A Guide to the Reading

If participants have not read this section already, read it aloud. Otherwise go on to "Questions for Application."

L uke ends his account of Jesus' early life with a pair of episodes set right where the story began—in the Jerusalem temple (1:8–9). Each scene features a visit to Israel's holy place, a finding of Jesus, amazement, and hints of future suffering.

The temple setting is no accident. It suggests that Jesus is growing up in the care of devout parents who observe the Mosaic law. Mary and Joseph have already complied with the requirement of circumcision (Luke 2:21). The first temple scene (Luke 2:22–38), which takes place when Jesus is forty days old, showcases their observance of other practices: the mother's purification after childbirth and the consecration of the firstborn son. Luke seems to have confused some details of these customs. Even so, his point is clear, especially since he mentions Mary and Joseph's fulfillment of the law five times (Luke 2:22, 23, 24, 27, 39). In scene two (Luke 2:41–50), the family is obeying the command to celebrate the annual Passover festival in Jerusalem. Since women and boys under thirteen were probably not obligated to make the pilgrimage, this is another indicator of the family's piety.

Active through the Mosaic law, God also works through the Holy Spirit, whose presence sweeps through both scenes. Mentioned three times in relation to Simeon (Luke 2:25–27), the Spirit is also the source of Anna's prophetic vocation (Luke 2:36). The Spirit guides these witnesses to Jesus at just the right time to just the right spot—no small feat, since the temple courtyard covered thirty-eight acres. If we read between the lines, it is also the Spirit who orchestrates the better-known finding of Jesus, when Mary and Joseph discover him in the process of amazing the temple teachers. Finally, Jesus' wisdom and understanding (Luke 2:40, 47, 52) are obviously from the Holy Spirit.

Scholars point out that "righteous and devout" Simeon (Luke 2:25) symbolizes the Mosaic law and Anna represents Israel's prophetic tradition. Those of us who have a tendency to view spirit and law as two necessarily warring entities—pitting obedience against inspiration, faithfulness against freedom, or institutional against spiritual—might want to linger over this picture of Anna and Simeon standing together in harmony.

Will Simeon survive the emotion of beholding and holding the Savior he and Anna have been awaiting (Luke 2:25–26, 36–38)? Indeed, his moving prayer (Luke 2:29–32) reads like a joyful farewell to earthly life. After faithfully keeping watch for the saving light now radiating to "all peoples," this "servant" is ready to go home and receive his Master's "Well done!"

But first, Simeon must sound a sober warning (Luke 2:34–35). Speaking to Mary alone (because Joseph will die before Jesus begins his ministry?), he prophesies that her Son will not be universally welcomed. A "sign that will be opposed," Jesus will expose people's hidden motivations and attachments in a way that leads them to take a stand for or against God's plan. This Prince of Peace brings a sword that cuts away lesser loyalties, causing division in the process (Luke 12:51–53; also Matthew 10:34).

Simeon foretells particular suffering for Mary. Twelve years later, the sword of division slices into her life. It is a moment of high anxiety: Jesus has been missing for three days. When Mary and Joseph finally discover him, we understand why her words convey astonishment and reproach (Luke 2:48). That Jesus answers with a mild rebuke—two questions indicating disappointment with his parents' lack of understanding (Luke 2:49)—is disconcerting. You should have known, he says, that "I must be in my Father's house"—or, as the Greek can also mean, "I must be involved in my Father's affairs" or "with those who belong to my Father's household." The words have a sting: Jesus must give priority to another Father's purposes, even when this cuts across his closest family ties.

Given Jesus' identity, his obedience to Joseph and Mary (Luke 2:51) is remarkable. But if this episode is any indicator of how Jesus will continue to increase in wisdom (Luke 2:52), we may suspect that the next eighteen years of "hidden life" will provide Mary and Joseph with numerous opportunities to rethink their parental expectations and adjust their plans. The final picture of Mary, mentally turning over her mysterious memories in order to penetrate their meaning (Luke 2:51), invites us to respond in kind as we seek to grasp Jesus' message for ourselves.

Questions for Application

40 minutes
Choose questions according to your interest and time.

1 Do you have a relationship with the Holy Spirit? What could you do to become more responsive and alert to the Spirit?

2 Simeon and Anna watched and prayed for God's "consolation" and "redemption" to come into the world (Luke 2:25, 38). What steps can a person take to move from self-centered prayer to prayer that encompasses "all peoples" (Luke 2:31)?

3 Jesus gives priority to obeying his heavenly Father while also showing proper obedience to Joseph and Mary. How might his example help you to establish your own priorities?

4 Do you sometimes imagine that you'd have an easier time understanding God's ways if only you could have been in Nazareth during Jesus' earthly years? What does Luke 2:50 suggest about this attitude?

5 For personal reflection: Reflect on your reading of Matthew's and Luke's presentations of Jesus' coming into our world. Which scenes in particular touched you? Keep pondering them, as Mary did, giving them time to bear fruit. Describing her approach, Bede wrote: "Nothing of what was said or done by Jesus fell idly on her mind. As before, when she conceived the Word itself in her womb, so now does she hold within her his ways and words, cherishing them as it were in her heart. That which she now beholds in the present, she waits to have revealed with greater clarity in the future."

A prayerful reading of the New Testament should normally leave us with a sense of wonder. Like Jesus' father and mother, we have been addressed by God's word and we marvel at what has been said (Luke 2:29–33). We may not have understood, . . . but with Mary we keep everything in our heart (Luke 2:51).

Eugene LaVerdiere, S.S.S., *The New Testament in the Life of the Church*

Approach to Prayer

15 minutes
Use this approach—or create your own!

◆ Silently or in a short group-sharing time, or both, express your desire to follow Simeon and Anna's example of watching and waiting for the Lord . . . Mary's example of reflecting on his words . . . Mary and Joseph's example of openness to whatever new horizons the Holy Spirit may reveal . . .

End by praying Psalm 130:5–7:

I wait for the LORD, my soul
      waits,
   and in his word I hope;
my soul waits for the LORD
   more than those who watch
      for the morning,
   more than those who watch
      for the morning.

O Israel, hope in the LORD!
   For with the LORD there is
      steadfast love,
   and with him is great power to
      redeem.

Saints in the Making

Hidden Lives of Nazareth

This section is a supplement for individual reading.

M any people have felt drawn to reflect on the holy family's "hidden years" in Nazareth. Charles de Foucauld went one step better. Converted from his bon vivant ways in 1886, he sought a hidden life of prayer in a Trappist monastery in his native France, then in a remote monastery in Syria, and finally in Nazareth. The "hidden life," says his biographer Jean-François Six, was "the essence of his spirituality—to replicate the life of Jesus at Nazareth." De Foucauld lived there from 1897 to 1900, working as a handyman at a convent of Poor Clare nuns. There, Six reports, "he filled notebook after notebook with meditations on the Gospels." In this excerpt, de Foucauld imagines Jesus explaining why he chose to spend most of his life in the obscurity of Nazareth.

It was for your sake I went there, *for love of you.* What was the meaning of that part of my life? I led it for your instruction. I instructed you continually for thirty years, not in words, but by my silence and example. . . . I was teaching you primarily that it is possible to do good to men—great good, infinite good, divine good—without using words, without preaching, without fuss, but by silence and by giving them a good example. . . . The example of devotion, of duty towards God lovingly fulfilled, and goodness towards all men, loving kindness to those about one and domestic duties fulfilled in holiness. The example of poverty, lowliness . . . the obscurity of a life hidden in God, a life of prayer, penance and withdrawal . . . buried deep in him. I was teaching you to live by the labor of your own hands, so as to be a burden on no one and to have something to give to the poor.

Charles de Foucauld eventually became a hermit in the Sahara. Still, he dreamed of attracting others who would live the spirit of Nazareth with him and be a quietly evangelistic presence, "drawing unbelievers to the faith by their example, goodness, and friendship." Though about fifty people committed themselves to following his "Gospel counsels," no one was living with him when he was murdered by Moroccan nationalists on December 1, 1916. Today, however, de Foucauld's ideals live on in the Little Brothers and Little Sisters of Jesus and other religious congregations and associations inspired by his example.

The Message of the Crib Is the Message of the Cross

Along with the joy that accompanies the birth of every child comes the sobering realization that infants make radical demands. Totally absorbed in their processes of ingestion, digestion, and elimination, they struggle for life—and leave their parents struggling for breathing room!

The Child in the manger makes even more radical demands. Do we notice them? Dietrich Bonhoeffer, a German Lutheran theologian who was executed by the Nazis, thought not: "We are indifferent to the message, taking only the pleasant and agreeable out of it and forgetting the serious aspect, that the God of the world draws near to the people of our little earth and lays claim to us."

The following excerpts come from two people who were very much attuned to both the glad and the grave tidings of Christmas. The first is from Dorothy Day, who cofounded the Catholic Worker lay movement in New York in 1933.

In Christ's human life there were always a few who made up for the neglect of the crowd. The shepherds did it; their hurrying to the crib atoned for the people who would flee from Christ. The wise men did it; their journey across the world made up for those who refused to stir one hand's breadth from the routine of their lives to go to Christ. . . . We can do it too, exactly as they did. We are not born too late. We do it by seeing Christ and serving Christ in friends and strangers, in everyone we come in contact with. . . .

Did you give me food when I was hungry? Did you give me something to drink when I was thirsty? Did you take me in when I was homeless and a stranger? Did you give me clothes when my own were all rags? Did you come to see me when I was sick or in prison or in trouble?

And to those who say, aghast, that they never had a chance to do such a thing, that they lived two thousand years too late, he will say again that they had the chance of knowing all their lives that if these things were done for the very least of his brethren, they were done for him. . . . [B]ecause they are Christ, asking us to find room for him exactly as he did at the first Christmas.

The following thoughts are from Sister Teresa Benedicta a Cruce ("Blessed by the Cross"), better known as Edith Stein. A German Carmelite, she also perished under the Nazi regime, in 1942, and was canonized in 1998.

The Son of the eternal Father descended from the glory of heaven because the mystery of iniquity had shrouded the earth in the darkness of night. This is the bitterly serious truth which ought not to be obscured by the poetic charm of the Child in the manger. The mystery of the Incarnation is closely linked to the mystery of iniquity. The night of sin appears all the more black and uncanny against the Light that comes down from heaven.

The Child in the manger stretches out his small hands, and his smile seems to say even now . . . "Come to me, all you that labor and are burdened." The poor shepherds have followed his call. . . . The kings from the faraway East followed the marvelous star with the same simple faith. On them all, the hands of the Child poured the dew of his grace, and they "rejoiced with exceeding great joy."

These hands give and demand at the same time. You wise men, lay down your wisdom and become simple like children. You kings, give your crowns and your treasures and bow humbly before the King of kings. Do not hesitate to take upon yourselves the sufferings and hardships his service entails. . . . These Child's hands say "Follow me," just as later the lips of the Man will say it. . . .

Those kneeling around the crib are figures of light: . . . the trustful shepherds, the humble kings . . . all those who have followed the call of the Lord. They are opposed by the night of incomprehensible obstinacy and blindness: the scribes, who know indeed when and where the Savior of the world is to be born, but who will not draw the conclusion: "Let us go to Bethlehem"; King Herod, who would kill the Lord of Life.

Ways part before the Child in the manger. He is the King of kings, the Lord of life and death. He speaks his "Follow me!" and if one is not for him, he is against him. He speaks also to us, and asks us to choose between light and darkness.

Suggestions for Bible Discussion Groups

Like a camping trip, a Bible discussion group works best if you agree on where you're going and how you intend to get there. Many groups use their first meeting to talk over such questions and reach a consensus. Here is a checklist of issues, with bits of advice from people who have experience in Bible discussions. (A planning discussion will go more smoothly if the leaders have thought through the following issues beforehand.)

Agree on your purpose. Are you getting together to gain wisdom and direction for your lives? to finally get acquainted with the Bible? to support one another in following Christ? to encourage those who are exploring—or reexploring—the Church? for other reasons?

Agree on attitudes. For example: "We're all beginners here." "We're here to help one another understand and respond to God's word." "We're not here to offer counseling or direction to one another." "We want to read Scripture prayerfully." What do *you* wish to emphasize? Make it explicit!

Agree on ground rules. Barbara J. Fleischer, in her useful book *Facilitating for Growth,* recommends that a group clearly state its approach to the following:

- *Preparation.* Do we agree to read the material and prepare answers to the questions before each meeting?
- *Attendance.* What kind of priority will we give to our meetings?
- *Self-revelation.* Are we willing to help the others in the group gradually get to know us—our weaknesses as well as our strengths, our needs as well as our gifts?
- *Listening.* Will we commit ourselves to listening to one another?
- *Confidentiality.* Will we keep everything that is shared *with* the group *in* the group?
- *Discretion.* Will we refrain from sharing about the faults and sins of people who are not in the group?
- *Encouragement and support.* Will we give as well as receive?
- *Participation.* Will we give each person the time and opportunity to make a contribution?

You could probably take a pen and draw a circle around *listening* and *confidentiality.* Those two points are especially important.

The following items could be added to Fleischer's list:

◆ *Relationship with parish.* Is our group part of the adult faith-formation program? independent but operating with the express approval of the pastor? not a parish-based group?

◆ *New members.* Will we let new members join us once we have begun the six weeks of discussions?

Agree on housekeeping.

◆ *When will we meet?*

◆ *How often will we meet?* Meeting weekly or every other week is best if you can manage it. William Riley remarks, "Meetings once a month are too distant from each other for the threads of the last session not to be lost" *(The Bible Study Group: An Owner's Manual).*

◆ *How long will meetings run?*

◆ *Where will we meet?*

◆ *Is any setup needed?* Christine Dodd writes that "the problem with meeting in a place like a church hall is that it can be very soul-destroying," given the cold, impersonal feel of many church facilities. If you have to meet in a church facility, Dodd recommends doing something to make the area homey *(Making Scripture Work).*

◆ *Who will host the meetings?* Leaders and hosts are not necessarily the same people.

◆ *Will we have refreshments?* Who will provide them?

◆ *What about child care?* Most experienced leaders of Bible discussion groups discourage bringing infants or other children to adult Bible discussions.

Agree on leadership. You need someone to facilitate— to keep the discussion on track, to see that everyone has a chance to speak, to help the group stay on schedule. Rena Duff, editor of the newsletter *Sharing God's Word Today,* recommends having two or three people take turns leading the discussions.

It's okay if the leader is not an expert on the Bible. You have this booklet, and if questions come up that no one can answer, you can delegate a participant to do a little research between meetings. It's important for the leader to set an example of listening, to draw out the quieter members (and occasionally restrain the more vocal ones), to move the group on when it gets stuck, to remind the members of their agreements, and to summarize what the group is accomplishing.

Bible discussion is an opportunity to experience the fulfillment of Jesus' promise "Where two or three are gathered in my name, I am there among them" (Matthew 18:20). Put your discussion group in Jesus' hands. Pray for the guidance of the Spirit. And have a great time exploring God's word together!

Suggestions for Individuals

Y ou can use this booklet just as well for individual study as for group discussion. While discussing the Bible with other people can be a rich experience, there are advantages to reading on your own. For example:

◆ You can focus on the points that interest you most.

◆ You can go at your own pace.

◆ You can be completely relaxed and unashamedly honest in your answers to all the questions, since you don't have to share them with anyone!

   My suggestions for using this booklet on your own are these:

◆ Don't skip the Questions to Begin. The questions can help you as an individual reader warm up to the topic of the reading.

◆ Take your time on the Questions for Careful Reading and Questions for Application. While a group will probably not have enough time to work on all the questions, you can allow yourself the time to consider all of them if you are using the booklet by yourself.

◆ After reading the Guide to the Reading, go back and reread the Scripture text before answering the Questions for Application.

◆ Take the time to look up all the parenthetical Scripture references in the introduction, the Guides to the Readings, and the other material.

◆ Since you control the pace, give yourself plenty of opportunities to reflect on the meaning of the Gospels for you. Let your reading be an opportunity for these words to become God's words to you.

Bibles

The following editions of the Bible contain the full set of biblical books recognized by the Catholic Church, along with a great deal of useful explanatory material:

- The Catholic Study Bible (Oxford University Press), which uses the text of the New American Bible
- The Catholic Bible: Personal Study Edition (Oxford University Press), which also uses the text of the New American Bible
- The New Jerusalem Bible, the regular (not the reader's) edition (Doubleday)

Books

- Raymond E. Brown, S.S., *The Birth of the Messiah: A Commentary on the Infancy Narratives in the Gospels of Matthew and Luke,* Anchor Bible Reference Library (New York: Doubleday, 1993).
- Joseph A. Fitzmyer, S.J., *The Gospel according to Luke, I–IX: Introduction, Translation, and Notes,* Anchor Bible, vol. 28 (New York: Doubleday, 1981).
- Joel B. Green, *The Gospel of Luke,* New International Commentary on the New Testament (Grand Rapids, Mich.: William B. Eerdmans, 1997).
- Eugene LaVerdiere, S.S.S., *Luke,* New Testament Message, vol. 5 (Wilmington, Del.: Michael Glazier, 1980).
- George T. Montague, S.M., *Companion God: A Cross-Cultural Commentary on the Gospel of Matthew* (New York: Paulist Press, 1989).

How has Scripture had an impact on your life? Was this booklet helpful to you in your study of the Bible? Please send comments, suggestions, and personal experiences to Kevin Perrotta, General Editor, Trade Editorial Department, Loyola Press, 3441 N. Ashland Ave., Chicago, IL 60657.